The Healing Companion

By Glynda Lomax

This book is dedicated to my King and Savior, Jesus Christ of Nazareth, without Whom I would be nothing, and without Whose sacrifice, I could not be eternally healed.

Thank You, Jesus. I love You.

Glynda

After a writing marathon of many months, I finally completed *The Wilderness Companion* in March of 2012. About a week later, God gave me a vision of books - three books, of which *The Wilderness Companion* was the first. This book, *The Healing Companion*, is the second book in the three-book series. The third book I saw was *The Grief Companion*.

Illness can be a lonely business, and a fearful one.

It is my goal with *The Healing Companion* to offer a healing book of a different kind, more of a user-friendly how-to manual to help you walk out your healing journey, and not feel so alone while doing it.

In this book, you will walk with me step-by-step through how I sought healing and the things God taught me along the way. You will see how He completely healed me from all the effects of a hemorrhagic stroke that nearly killed me, along with many recurring health problems, and constant, excruciating pain. I had hurt for so long, I had really given up hope that I would ever be completely well.

But today I AM completely well, and praising our mighty God because of it.

You can be, too.

May God mightily bless you as you read this book and walk out your own healing journey.

Glynda Lomax

Me – Spring 2012, Just before my healing journey began

CHAPTER 1 - DO YOU TRUST ME?

Do you trust Me to heal you?

It was March 12, 2012 and I had just walked into my bedroom to put something away when the Lord spoke to me, out of the blue. I had not been praying at the time, so it caught me by surprise somewhat.

Do you trust Me to heal you?

Yes, Lord, I trust You. Of course I trust You.

I tried hard not to panic. *Why was He asking me that?*

He did not say why He asked me that question, but I pondered it for weeks. I had been studying healing because the Lord had told me to press in for revelation on it, that it was necessary for us to move forward with the work He wanted to do at Princeton.

Inside, I was more than a little bit concerned that I knew why He was asking me. Not because *He* wanted or needed assurance I trusted Him to heal me, but because He wanted *me* to know I trusted Him to heal me.

And think about it I did, as I continued studying healing every day.

Around that same time, the Lord showed me a vision during prayer of *The Wilderness Companion*. But He didn't show me just one book, He showed me three. A series.

I was overjoyed there would be more books like the first one, because the first one was being received so well, and seemed to be helping to build the faith of my brothers and sisters in Christ as they walked out their wilderness journeys.

Then He showed me one of the books was about healing.

Lord, I hope I'm not going to have to have some horrible disease to write that one!

Silence.

Even as I said that, I knew the best books were based on personal experience. Writers write best what they know, and I wondered for weeks after that day how well I would have to get to know sickness and disease in order to write about God's healing power. I had suffered a number of terrifying journeys into the wilderness before writing *The Wilderness Companion*.

I actually had no real revelation on healing, though I had prayed and seen miracles happen for others. I generally suffered through sickness, trudging off to the doctor, plunking down hundreds of dollars for doctor visits, and taking medicine to get well. I knew there was a better way, and I had read book after book about healing. I could see and believe it for others, but I didn't "get it" for me, which meant I had no revelation in that area yet.

For over two months, I had been experiencing pain in my left shoulder. Since I was experiencing a lot of back pain at that time,

I thought it was due to my spine being misaligned. After waking up one morning with extreme pain in the shoulder and so much pain in my back I could not walk correctly, I went to a chiropractor for an adjustment. I thought getting an adjustment would correct the shoulder problem as well. It hadn't. In fact, the shoulder pain had gotten worse.

The chiropractor had seen nothing on the x-ray that he felt should be causing so much pain in the shoulder and suggested I might need to have an MRI, something that was not even in the realm of possibility for me, having no health insurance, and MRI's costing hundreds of dollars. He prescribed mobility exercises and suggested ice packs to help with the pain.

The pain became more excruciating by the day. I wasn't sure what was going on, so I made a doctor's appointment, partly so I would at least know the name of what I needed to rebuke to get healed, and partly because I truly wanted a diagnosis.

Over the weeks that followed as I waited for the day of the doctor's appointment, I continued to try to keep the arm mobile. Sometimes it would stiffen up and not want to raise, and at other times it became very weak, making my hand tingle. I always associated those symptoms with bone misalignment, so I was really confused the symptoms were not related to that.

Lord, I'm doing everything I know to do, but this shoulder is still freezing up, and some days it hurts really bad. Please help!

Silence.

I began using Naproxen and capsaicin cream to dull the pain enough that I could keep writing. The Lord had assigned me to write a book about betrayal and I was also making notes on some future books He had shown me I would be writing. In addition, I had added a second radio show every week, and I was still maintaining the Wings of Prophecy site and my YouTube channel, so I had plenty to do, in spite of the fact I had stopped working outside the home months before at His direction.

As the days passed, I lost more range of motion and mobility in the shoulder, even though I was doing the prescribed exercises several times a day. I had to make accommodations in my position to style my waist-length hair or pull clothing over my head. I was reading healing articles and looking up scriptures several times a week, and I was confident I would be healed, so I worked with the immobility as best I could and kept going.

Later in March, the Lord spoke to me again.

My precious daughter, it is indeed My will and My plan that you be healed, but you have not been diligent to study My Word in this area to see what I have provided for you there. I do not hand revelation down to those who do not show themselves approved. Go now and show yourself approved before Me, and I will answer your prayer, that you may serve Me better in this way.

I'm sorry, Lord. I will try harder.

I had been distracted by many things as usual and was struggling to focus to any degree. I had been struggling more and more with a lack of focus for the last few years, and attributed it to my age, my usual stress level, and my constant drive to get more done. Sometimes it seemed the harder I pressed in, the less I could focus. I rebuked the enemy over and over, but the problem persisted.

Over the next several weeks, the pain in my left shoulder increased greatly. I prayed often for help with the pain and tried to be diligent about studying the healing scriptures as the Lord had instructed me. With my schedule, it was difficult to do everything already, and adding one more thing was not helping. In addition, I noticed I was losing the ability to grip very well with the hand on my left side. During times when the pain was severe, I would often drop things. I had to compensate and make up the difference with my right hand.

The night of April 10th, during worship, the Lord spoke to me again.

Your healing will manifest soon. I want you to press in - fight the enemy for it! I will teach you and give you revelation as you do this. Otherwise, you shall not be able to write The Healing Companion. You must know and experience pain firsthand. You cannot write the book without pressing in. Many thousands shall be helped and healed through this book in a time when medical help shall be scarce and hard to come by.

The next night, He spoke again during my prayer time.

Learn from those who have gone before you and mastered healing. Practice the steps they did and listen for My voice and I will reveal to you new information not yet revealed for The Healing Companion. Your pain will be intense, but short-lived compared to many others. It is only that your testimony may ring true. You must know the enemy you fight in order to teach others. It shall be a short process for you, as it is only for this book. From then on, you shall walk in health.

The devil will try to talk you into giving up the fight daughter, but you forfeit the rewards of good health and writing this book if you do, also the rewards in heaven from the many lives it touched and how I will be glorified through it. Do not disappoint Me in this. Many thousands will suffer needlessly if you are unwilling to complete this task.

When the pain becomes much, press in harder! Call out My Name, worship Me, praise Me for the result. I promise you the duration will be short if you will fight hard and study others and press in for it.

The enemy does not want you writing these books because he knows and sees the lives they touch for My glory.

If you back down from healing, he will attack you harder with disease.

There is no turning back after this. This healing is truly My will for you, but you must stand for it and press in to receive it, but then it is yours forever. You only have to do this once. Set your face like flint and do not back down until you receive your complete healing. If you do, he will strike you. Now that you have begun your healing journey, you must complete it or your pain will be even worse, for the enemy will attack you again and again in any area where your understanding in My Word is not strong.

Proceed boldly, knowing I have already healed you. You are My child and there is nothing for you to fear. Stand and boldly confess My Word over your body and over your life, for I stand beside you ready to perform it!

When the Lord told me the enemy would attack me harder if I backed down, I knew I had to choose whether I would view that as a cause for panic or a call to action. Never one to quit and run, I started preparing to armor up for the fight.

When He spoke to me to study those who have gone before me and been healed, I saw Dodie Osteen in my spirit, along with others such as Kenneth Copeland. I began gathering my healing books and resources so I could study them. I had heard many of their testimonies. Dodie's small book, *Healed of Cancer*, was my favorite healing book because it was easy to read and had scripture references in the back to confess. Two weeks or less from death in 1981, she beat liver cancer to death with the sword of the spirit and is still alive today, laying hands on others and helping them receive their healing.

I knew what the Lord meant when He said the enemy would attack me harder if I backed down. Any area the enemy sees your weakness in, or that you are unwilling to fight in, he will not relent from.

He will attack you again and again in that area until he defeats you. I knew there was no direction for me to go but forward, or the price I would pay would be a big one. When the Lord said the enemy would strike me if I backed down, I saw a flash vision of a coiled rattlesnake striking in my spirit. I knew from what I saw that meant he would try to kill me. I tried at all times to keep every door closed to the enemy. He is always out there, just waiting for his chance to strike at all of God's People.

As I pressed in to the Word of God more and more in days following to get the revelation I knew would heal my body forever, I struggled with my daily choices. For years prior to pressing in, I regularly took over-the-counter painkillers as I needed them for severe back pain. I had also begun using capsaicin cream numerous times per day, a topical anesthetic that helped ease the pain in my shoulder enough that I could perform my daily tasks.

I began to wake up all during the night with the pain in my shoulder so intense it made resting nearly impossible.

The Naproxen and capsaicin cream did not take away the pain, but they helped dull it enough I could rest at least some at night and function during the day.

Within weeks it became so severe, they barely touched it. I quickly found myself applying the cream six or more times a day, and I knew the tube said four was the maximum. I just wasn't sure how else to handle the pain.

Lord, I'm not sure what to do here. I don't want to take the painkillers if taking them means I lack faith, but this really hurts.

Silence.

I wanted to do the right thing, to please God, and I also wanted to be completely healed. Should I forego any pain relief to speed up the process? Would it do that or just make me more miserable while I pressed in?

I decided to try it.

The pain quickly became so severe that it made hours of misery feel like days as I fought the urge to use the painkillers over the following days, unsure which was the right thing to do.

I had never suffered a severe illness, though I had dealt with many smaller ones over the years. A year never passed that I was not in the doctor's office at least three or four times, so sick I could barely hold my head up. If the enemy was putting illness on me, I planned to put a stop to it once and for all.

How could I ever hope to pray for the healing of others if I could not even understand healing enough to receive it for myself?

Soon after, the pain began to spread to my other shoulder. I was pretty sure that was not a good sign. It made my daily routines so much more difficult having to fight weakness in both arms and hands at the same time. Thank God, it wasn't bad yet in the right one. Still, even simple daily tasks became huge challenges because of it.

One night, my frustration mounted as I struggled to open a jar. I had already lost much of the gripping power in my left hand, but thought if I could use my handy jar opening gadget that I could open it anyhow. I couldn't. I tried tapping it, using a towel on it, praying over it, and yelling at it, but nothing worked. I sat in the floor, repeating every method over and over, until, after five long minutes, I finally managed to get it open.

Not being able to open a jar seems like a small thing, but if you are single and live alone, it can become a very big thing. Having taken care of myself for so many years, the thought of not being able to terrified me, partly because there was no one else to do it, but also because I didn't want anyone else to have to.

What would it be like in another month? Another year? At this pace, I wasn't sure what other terrible surprises this new condition had in store for me, whatever it was.

Lord, this can't continue. I have to get healed!

Silence.

Early the next afternoon, the increasing pain in my shoulders was agonizing. Every movement brought more pain, and I could barely use my arms, even though I had worked hard to keep them mobile by doing my prescribed exercises several times a day. I stared at the bottle of Naproxen. Should I take it? Did it mean I lacked faith if I tried to silence the pain screaming through my arms?

I hurt so badly I had not been able to concentrate for days, and I was accomplishing very little each day while trying to endure it. I had decided to try foregoing painkillers, and just get the healing over with, but I was finding it difficult to function when even the smallest movement caused a major increase in my pain level.

Not only had the increasing pain reached a new level as all the anti-inflammatories wore off, but it was seriously affecting my hands. I would make my way slowly into the kitchen and attempt to fix something to eat and when I finished, find it lying on the floor where I'd dropped it because of my weak grip.

Earlier that day, I had dropped a diet dinner straight out of the microwave, and it had splattered all over my dress and the kitchen floor. I wanted to cry. I hadn't realized I had lost that much of the gripping power in my right hand. Would I lose my ability to type as well? How would I write books if I could not type?

One evening soon after, I was sitting at my computer, trying to work in spite of the searing pain that had become my constant companion, when I realized it had gone on so long that I was gritting my teeth trying to endure it. My shoulders felt like they had spikes driven through them and I was not faring well trying to walk out the pain and keep up with my daily tasks.

Having not accomplished anything of significance for days, I decided the over-the-counter painkillers were probably going to be necessary if I wanted to keep functioning as I walked out my healing journey, and I began taking them again.

Either way, I knew what I had to do to see my healing manifest, so

I might as well make it as bearable as possible. My faith was not affected one way or the other by taking them. The painkillers did not come anywhere near killing all the pain, they merely took the edge off it enough that I could perform my daily tasks.

One morning just days later, I was in my kitchen preparing oatmeal. Reaching up to take something off a shelf, I accidentally knocked over a canister of tea bags next to it. Instinctively, I reached out to grab the falling canister.....with my left arm. It took me less than one full second to regret that move as pain shot down my arm so intense, I almost blacked out. I dropped to my knees on the floor, clutching my arm, trying not to be sick, and crawled to the refrigerator for an ice pack. I slammed the ice pack down on the shoulder and began confessing every healing scripture I knew over and over as I fought the urge to be sick.

The ice pack helped enough that I didn't scream from the pain and alarm the entire neighborhood, but I felt the inflammation increasing and within minutes, I could not grip anything at all with that hand.

45 minutes later, I was still shaking from the trauma of such intense pain. Only once before in my life could I remember ever feeling pain so intense I nearly blacked out, and it was so bad then that I had almost dialed 911.

It was clear this was not going to be an easy journey.

At times when the pain was so severe, or when my lack of mobility was especially tedious and keeping me from doing my many daily tasks, I was almost overcome with hopelessness. I knew the Lord wanted me to walk in health. I knew He had spoken to me over and over that I needed to press in to get a revelation on healing so I would no longer have to deal with pain or sickness, but every time I would press in just long enough the pain left, then something else would take priority.

This time I knew without asking that would not be the case. I had to keep pressing in. I had to get a true understanding of why I was entitled to be healed, and I would have to fight the enemy every time the symptoms appeared. At the moment, they were constant, but I had a doctor's appointment in two days.

Having been without health insurance for over eight years, I had bypassed getting yearly checkups. So much had happened in my life over those eight years, that I stayed in react mode most of the time, spending little time on anything preventative, other than taking vitamins and numerous herbal supplements daily. I prayed the doctor would be able to tell me what was causing the intense pain and debilitation in my arms.

When the day of my doctor visit finally arrived, she poked and prodded around the left shoulder and advised she believed it was some sort of soft tissue problem. She did some pressure point therapy on it, during which she pressed so long and hard on the points that I was sure I would be bruised, but which did nothing to relieve the pain.

I left her office completely disappointed at her lack of diagnosis. I felt she had failed to even show compassion for the intensity of pain I was suffering so horribly from. I was not asking for painkillers, I just wanted to know why I was hurting so badly. She seemed to have no idea how to even diagnose me. I wondered how she had gotten her medical license.

I began to realize that when God wants to teach you something, He won't allow you to solve your problem any other way. I tried to fight the hopelessness rising up in me again as I thought of more days and nights of intense pain and reduced mobility. I had to get healed, that was all there was to it.

Just days later near the end of April, the pain suddenly began to increase in my right shoulder. It was already very pronounced in my left one from the night before, the place I most often felt it. It intensified rapidly.

Within five minutes, I could not grip anything at all with my right hand and the muscles in the top half of my arm began going into spasms. I had no idea what was wrong, only that it hurt horribly. I had learned to use whichever arm hurt the least to get things done as I moved through my days, but I had no idea what to do if they both hurt really bad at the same time, because I could not grip anything or raise them above shoulder level when the pain was severe.

I had become busy again over the past few days, and stopped confessing my healing and studying healing in the Word, though I was still listening to the recording I had made of healing scriptures all night almost every night as I slept, and I would listen to them in the mornings as I laid in bed waking up, occasionally quoting this one or that one during the day.

There is a huge difference between hearing scriptures and speaking them out loud when you are believing for a promise of God to manifest in your life. That difference cannot be over-emphasized.

Faith *comes* by hearing the Word (Romans 10:17), but it is only *released* by speaking it out loud (Mark 11:23).

Romans 10:17

So then faith cometh by hearing, and hearing by the Word of God.

Mark 11:23

For verily I say unto you, That whosoever shall say unto this mountain, Be thou removed, and be thou cast into the sea; and shall not doubt in his heart, but shall believe that those things which he saith shall come to pass; he shall have whatsoever he saith.

I knew this truth, but had let other things creep into my schedule and take over the time I usually spent working on pressing in. Now I was beginning to feel the full effect of what could happen if I did not get back to work studying healing for the full manifestation in my body.

With a big stack of mail and a package in my good hand, I struggled that evening to get out the door to go to the Post Office. With only my left hand working, it was a fight getting up into my pickup and driving.

Lord, if both my shoulders ever do this on the same day, I'm in big trouble! I won't even be able to dress myself, much less drive!

Silence.

He hadn't answered, but I had not expected Him to. He had told me to press in and there I was, not obeying again.

I knew I would pay the price if I did not get in line with what He had told me to do. I promised myself I would get back into the Word studying healing and make time to confess my healing scriptures out loud every day. I could not afford for the pain and debilitation to increase. How would I take care of myself if my arms stopped working, with no job and no health insurance? The thought was more than frightening.

The following morning, I awoke with the pain still in both shoulders. In my left side, it extended beyond my elbow, making every movement more painful. My right shoulder was barely movable. The pain level was so high, I had awakened after only four hours sleep feeling nauseous from all the painkillers I had taken the night before.

Getting out of bed very slowly, I struggled to dress myself, finally choosing a long simple pullover dress. I was not looking forward to another day of pain and struggling through my daily tasks.

How did people survive years of such terrible pain and

23

debilitation? What happened to the ones who lived alone and could not do all their daily tasks? My heart broke at the thought of anyone fighting such a battle on their own, especially the elderly.

Sitting at my desk a little while later, I tried to apply the capsaicin cream to my shoulders to ease the pain, only to find I could barely reach the tip of either one due to increased immobility.

It was clear this was not going to be a fun day and very likely not a fun journey either, for that matter. I decided I would try to focus on the good in my situation.

The Lord had told me I would only have to fight this battle once, and that I would walk in good health after it was over. I really wanted to be healthy, so I began rejoicing that I soon would be. He had told me the book I was writing about healing would help thousands of others receive their own healing, so I rejoiced greatly over that. Though the pain was intense, it was pain with a purpose. It would help my brothers and sisters in Christ so they would not also have to hurt.

As an added benefit, such intense pain had decreased my appetite dramatically, so it was likely I would lose the extra 30 lbs. I was carrying more quickly, and that was also something to rejoice about.

In addition, the Lord had told me to confess boldly, knowing He has already healed me. I determined this would be one battle the enemy would lose, once and for all. I already knew it would be a hard one, but I also knew I could be relentless in pressing in when I knew something was mine.

This was one time I would have no other choice. The pain and immobility were threatening to change my life forever and I was not willing to let it do that. I could not allow any disability to stop me from fulfilling God's purposes in my life. That was my first priority.

I fought back tears as the morning drug on, and the pain kept increasing. I had learned sitting in the sun for 20 minutes a day helped my pain level, so I decided I would begin a daily routine of sitting outside in the sun and confessing my healing. If I combined the two, it would help me keep my confession time for that part of the day. My goal was to begin confessing them at least three times a day, just as I would take medicine for an ailment. I would also listen to them on CD on low volume during the day as much as possible, and at night while I slept. I needed God's Word on healing to get deep down into my spirit, and the sooner, the better.

Every book I had ever read on healing said we are already healed by the stripes of Jesus. I knew the Word of God said I was healed, but when I looked at my body, I didn't see healing, I saw sickness and pain. In order to see my healing manifest in my body, I knew I would need more than just head knowledge that the scriptures said I was healed. I needed *understanding*.

As we study and meditate on the Word of God, the Lord rewards us with understanding - the revelation of the true meaning behind a scripture. Sometimes when I am reading the Word, a scripture will almost appear to jump off the page or appear illuminated to me as He shows me *in my spirit* (not just in my mind) what that part of His Word means. I knew I needed a revelation of His truth where healing was concerned. Just knowing in my head that I was supposed to be healed wasn't bringing any results. I needed His Word deep in my spirit if I was going to actually see my healing manifest.

Every believer needs to study the Word of God to see what He has provided for them there in the way of healing. **You won't get healed using someone else's understanding, you have to get your own.** The reason is because if you try to manifest healing using someone else's revelation, you're running on head knowledge and you won't see any results from head knowledge.

Head knowledge means you know what the scripture says, but have no real revelation or understanding at a spiritual level of why that promise is yours to claim. You can't get revelation with your head, the Holy Spirit must reveal these truths to you. This revelation will only come to you as it did to me, when you study to show yourself approved.

A great way to start a study like this is by choosing a healing scripture and beginning to just repeat it over and over in your mind, or by speaking it, and just think about it as you go about your day. Maybe write it on a card and look at it and read it throughout the day. The most important part of this process is going over and over it in your mind. This is what it means to meditate on scripture, and if you will do it all day, you will receive tremendous revelation on that scripture. But you must be diligent about it. You can't just think about it once or twice and expect to receive some mighty revelation.

Another way to receive revelation is to break the scriptures down, word by word, using an Exhaustive Strong's Concordance, which provides the definitions of the original languages the books of the Bible were written in, indexed in English. Every word in one language does not translate exactly into another language, so some scriptures have meanings not immediately apparent in English. This is the way we uncover these meanings.

Isaiah 53:4-5 - He is despised and rejected of men; a man of sorrows, and acquainted with grief: and we hid as it were our faces from him; he was despised, and we esteemed him not.

53:4 Surely he hath borne our griefs, and carried our sorrows: yet we did esteem him stricken, smitten of God, and afflicted.

Isaiah 53:4 is the scripture that spoke to me most strongly about the fact that I was healed and not supposed to be sick or in pain, and it was the one I quoted again and again in pressing in to see the full manifestation of healing in my body.

When I began to study Isaiah 53:4, there were several things about it that spoke to me. One was that the word translated borne in this verse literally means *to carry away.*

It means Jesus carried away our griefs, and the word translated griefs means *sickness and diseases.* So Jesus carried away our sickness and diseases.

Once a week, I put my heavy garbage cart out by the curb for pickup. A service comes by and picks up the bin and takes the trash to where it needs to go.

Do I need to go out there and carry the same trash? No.

Why?

Because someone else *carried it away for me.*

Jesus carried away our sickness and diseases when He bore our sins on the cross. They're gone. He carried those burdens away. That means we don't also have to carry them down here.

If my waste management service tried to put that garbage back on me and tell me I had to carry it away myself, I would have to contradict them, because that garbage isn't mine to carry. That service is provided to me. It's already paid for.

Sickness and disease isn't ours to carry, either.

The word translated sorrows in this verse means grief, pain or sorrow. It comes from a root word that literally means "to feel pain."

So vs. 4 also shows that Jesus carried all our pain, as well as our griefs and sorrows. That means we don't have to carry those, either. **This verse showed me that pain was trespassing on my body, and I didn't have to stand for it any more.**

Isaiah 53:5 says with his stripes, we are healed. Now look at 1 Peter 2:24, below. it says by whose stripes we *were* healed. Did you see that? The Old Testament said *are healed*, the New Testament says *were healed*. **That means when the New Covenant came, our healing came with it. We've already been healed through Jesus' death on the Cross.**

I Peter 2:24 - Who his own self bare our sins in his own body on the tree, that we, being dead to sins, should live unto righteousness: by whose stripes ye were healed

---

ABRAHAM'S FAITH

Romans 4:19-20

And being not weak in faith, he considered not his own body now dead, when he was about an hundred years old, neither yet the deadness of Sarah's womb: He staggered not at the promise of God through unbelief; but was strong in faith, giving glory to God;

Abraham did not consider the circumstances of his own body, he did not listen to the reports of his friends - he listened only to the words of his God, and he meditated on *those*.

He didn't let anyone else's words or opinions get him into unbelief, he just kept on moving forward.

If we will not consider the circumstances (symptoms) of our bodies, if we will not listen to the prognosis of our doctors (with all due respect, they deal in FACT, but our God deals in TRUTH, which trumps fact *every time*), if we will not listen to the dire predictions of our friends or give heed to the worried looks of our family…if we listen only to what the Word of God says about us – that we **were** healed, if we will meditate only on His Words, we will soon see our circumstances and symptoms matching up with His Word.

Our faith and our words have great power. Whichever one we believe – sickness or His Word, that is the one that will prevail.

Deuteronomy 7:15 - And the LORD will take away from thee all sickness, and will put none of the evil diseases of Egypt, which thou knowest, upon thee; but will lay them upon all them that hate thee.

2 Timothy 1:7 - For God hath not given us the spirit of fear; but of power, and of love, and of a sound mind.

Isaiah 41:10 - Fear thou not; for I am with thee: be not dismayed; for I am thy God: I will strengthen thee; yea, I will help thee; yea, I will uphold thee with the right hand of my righteousness.

Isaiah 54:17 - No weapon that is formed against thee shall prosper; and every tongue that shall rise against thee in judgment thou shalt condemn. This is the heritage of the servants of the LORD, and their righteousness is of me, saith the LORD.

Sickness, disease and pain are all weapons formed by the enemy. The enemy is judging you and saying you should be ill or in pain or have a disease and he is striking you with that. It's up to you to fight him on it. It's up to each of us to fight for our healing. Jesus bought it for us, but we have to stand up to the enemy and take it.

I John 4:4 - Ye are of God, little children, and have overcome them: because greater is he that is in you, than he that is in the world.

Joel 3:10 - let the weak say "I am strong."

Romans 8;31 - What shall we then say to these things? If God be for us, who can be against us?

Isaiah 40:31 - But they that wait upon the LORD shall renew their strength; they shall mount up with wings as eagles; they shall run, and not be weary; and they shall walk, and not faint.

Jeremiah 30:17 - For I will restore health unto thee, and I will heal thee of thy wounds, saith the LORD; because they called thee an Outcast, saying, This is Zion, whom no man seeketh after.

Isaiah 53:4-5 - 4 Surely he hath borne our griefs, and carried our sorrows: yet we did esteem him stricken, smitten of God, and afflicted.

5 But he was wounded for our transgressions, he was bruised for our iniquities: the chastisement of our peace was upon him; and with his stripes we are healed.

Jeremiah 33:6 - Behold, I will bring it health and cure, and I will cure them, and will reveal unto them the abundance of peace and truth.

Isaiah 58:8 - Then shall thy light break forth as the morning, and thine health shall spring forth speedily: and thy righteousness shall go before thee; the glory of the Lord shall be thy reward.

Psalm 41:3 - The LORD will strengthen him upon the bed of languishing: thou wilt make all his bed in his sickness. In the NASB, this verse is translated to say that the Lord will sustain him upon his sickbed and restore him to health. What an awesome promise!

Psalm 103:1-5 - Bless the LORD, O my soul: and all that is within me, bless his holy name.

2 Bless the LORD, O my soul, and forget not all his benefits:

3 Who forgiveth all thine iniquities; who healeth all thy diseases;

4 Who redeemeth thy life from destruction; who crowneth thee with lovingkindness and tender mercies;

5 Who satisfieth thy mouth with good things; so that thy youth is renewed like the eagle's.

Psalm 107:20 - He sent his word, and healed them, and delivered them from their destructions.

Psalm 118:17 - I shall not die, but live, and declare the works of the LORD.

Psalm 30:2 - O LORD my God, I cried unto thee, and thou hast healed me.

Psalm 35:27 - Let them shout for joy, and be glad, that favour my righteous cause: yea, let them say continually, Let the LORD be magnified, which hath pleasure in the prosperity of his servant.

Psalm 119:50 - My soul breaketh for the longing that it hath unto thy judgments at all times.

3 John 1:2 - Beloved, I wish above all things that thou mayest prosper and be in health, even as thy soul prospereth.

Jeremiah 17:14 - Heal me, O Lord, and I shall be healed; save me, and I shall be saved: for thou art my praise.

II Corinthians 1:20 - For all the promises of God in him are yea, and in him Amen, unto the glory of God by us.

Deuteronomy 30:19 - I call heaven and earth to record this day against you, that I have set before you life and death, blessing and cursing: therefore choose life, that both thou and thy seed may live:

Matthew 18:18 - Verily I say unto you, Whatsoever ye shall bind on earth shall be bound in heaven: and whatsoever ye shall loose on earth shall be loosed in heaven.

Mark 11:22-23 - And Jesus answering saith unto them, Have faith in God.

23 For verily I say unto you, That whosoever shall say unto this mountain, Be thou removed, and be thou cast into the sea; and shall not doubt in his heart, but shall believe that those things which he saith shall come to pass; he shall have whatsoever he saith.

This is especially important in the area of healing. **Make no mistake about it, Satan will try to gain control of your tongue, and if he can get it, he can steal your healing from right under your nose, because he can control your entire body through that one little member. Don't deceive yourself into thinking you can talk pain and sickness and walk in health. We get what we say.**

Hebrews 10:23 - Let us hold fast the profession of our faith without wavering; (for he is faithful that promised;)

*Hebrews 10:35 - **Cast not away therefore your confidence, which hath great recompence of reward.***

Our words have incredible power. The Bible says with our words we have the power to either bring blessing or cursing, and that we get what we say. The wise person will speak health and wellness, not sickness, pain and disease. This includes *not* going around saying you have this or that disease. Every time you claim it, you are decreeing it which establishes it.

Job 22:28

28 Thou shalt also decree a thing, and it shall be established unto thee: and the light shall shine upon thy ways.

Proverbs 18:21

Death and life are in the power of the tongue: and they that love it shall eat the fruit thereof.

James 3:2-6

2 For in many things we offend all. If any man offend not in word, the same is a perfect man, and able also to bridle the whole body.

3 Behold, we put bits in the horses' mouths, that they may obey us; and we turn about their whole body.

4 Behold also the ships, which though they be so great, and are driven of fierce winds, yet are they turned about with a very small helm, whithersoever the governor listeth.

5 Even so the tongue is a little member, and boasteth great things. Behold, how great a matter a little fire kindleth!

6 And the tongue is a fire, a world of iniquity: so is the tongue among our members, that it defileth the whole body, and setteth on fire the course of nature; and it is set on fire of hell.

Mark 11:23

For verily I say unto you, That whosoever shall say unto this mountain, Be thou removed, and be thou cast into the sea; and shall not doubt in his heart, but shall believe that those things which he saith shall come to pass; he shall have whatsoever he saith.

Proverbs 12:18

There is that speaketh like the piercings of a sword: but the tongue of the wise is health.

The world we live in is framed by the words of God. Our world is framed by *our* words.

My friend John Morgan, who has studied healing in depth and outlived the doctor's prognosis by years already, shared this with me, which I found to be very powerful:

"I believe Genesis, among other things, establishes what I call the Rule of Witnesses. There were three witnesses to the creation: the Father, Son, and Spirit. Later in the Bible, it tells us three interesting things in different places.

First, the Word of God is established in heaven.

Second, every Word of God is tested.

Third, everything must be established by two or three witnesses.

When we speak God's Word, a court is spiritually convened. The Word of God we spoke is a witness, already found to be a true witness. Our pain and symptoms are a witness, which we now know is a lying witness sent by the enemy.

Then we are called as a witness. Our testimony is examined to see if we are a true witness to the Word. This examination takes place over time in a period which the Bible calls endurance. If our words and actions are steadfast (the same as the Word of God we spoke), then we are found to be a true witness. The established Logos in heaven can then become a Rhema established in our physical realm."

I was laying in bed one night about to go to sleep, reading a book about healing, when I heard the Lord speak this to me, *"Say it and see it."*

Your healing battle will be won or lost through your words and whether you can see yourself healed in your mind.

Our words are a very important part of the healing battle, they may in fact be our biggest weapon after the revelation from the Word that we are, in fact, already healed. If our words are wrong, then they become Satan's biggest weapon *against* us. We become our own worst enemy. Healing is a war that is won in the spirit through battles fought in your mind and body.

Proverbs 12:18

There is that speaketh like the piercings of a sword: but the tongue of the wise is health.

The tongue of the wise is *health*. That means if we are wise, we will speak of our good health and not sickness or pain or weakness. I saw the truth of this rule played out in my Mother's life.

Although she was in a care home the last eight years of her life, up until the very end, she enjoyed mostly good health, other than the dementia she suffered.

I remember visiting her many times and her saying in the course of conversation, "I'm in excellent health!" The Lord showed me in my spirit when I was visiting her once that her constant confession of good health was the very reason why her health had not deteriorated completely. Not until the last two months of her life on earth did I hear her confess her health was failing. She was almost 88 years old when she passed into the arms of our Jesus. Her last words were a prayer to Him before she slipped into a coma near the end.

Our minds are to our bodies what the operating systems are to our computers. What a computer can do is based on what is programmed into it through the operating system. If you want it to do more, you upgrade, or renew, the operating system. You install new software. It's like giving the brains of the computer new abilities and instructions to follow. We are the same way - if we want our bodies to do more, we need to upgrade, or renew, our minds.

Romans 12:2

2 And be not conformed to this world: but be ye transformed by the renewing of your mind, that ye may prove what is that good, and acceptable, and perfect, will of God

Glynda Lomax

Mom and Me - 2007

The picture we see of ourselves in our minds or imaginations is of prime importance. The words we speak and the thoughts we entertain or think on create the images we see of ourselves. This is why it is so important we do not allow our minds to be programmed by our doctor's reports or our friends dire predictions of our health outcome, or their stories of what happened to so-and-so that had the same diagnosis. We choose which thoughts we will think on, and those thoughts dictate the state of our bodies. **The images in our minds instruct our brains to create what we see there.**

Our thoughts, what is in our hearts, also determines what comes out of our mouths. What comes out of our mouths also determines what happens to our bodies. **This is why Satan works so hard to feed you wicked imaginations and thoughts of doom, and to get you to talk about it.**

Romans 12:2

And be not conformed to this world: but be ye transformed by the renewing of your mind, that ye may prove what is that good, and acceptable, and perfect, will of God.

I had grown up being told I was a sickly child and that I would most likely always have poor health. It had never occurred to me growing up that the information I was told about my health was incorrect. Children believe what they are told. Now I saw the truth of what it was, the fearful opinion of a loving, worried Mom.

Mom and Me - 2011

It was up to me to tear down the lies the enemy had constructed in my soul through those lies and the only way to destroy lies is with the Sword of Truth - the Word of God spoken out loud.

The best news about this is, even if you are so ill you are bedridden, you can still speak the Word of God. The most imperative thing, though, is that you absolutely must have your own personal revelation from the Word of God that healing is your right as a child of the Most High God. **That** is what puts faith to your words and expectation in your heart.

The Word of God is like a powerful race car, but your faith is the fuel it must have to move forth powerfully.

2 Corinthians 12:9 - And he said unto me, My grace is sufficient for thee: for my strength is made perfect in weakness. Most gladly therefore will I rather glory in my infirmities, that the power of Christ may rest upon me.

Joel 3:10 - Beat your plowshares into swords and your pruninghooks into spears: let the weak say, I am strong.

Luke 12:32 - Fear not, little flock; for it is your Father's good pleasure to give you the kingdom.

Psalm 35:27 - Let them shout for joy, and be glad, that favour my righteous cause: yea, let them say continually, Let the Lord be magnified, which hath pleasure in the prosperity of his servant.

Jeremiah 29:11 - For I know the thoughts that I think toward you, saith the Lord, thoughts of peace, and not of evil, to give you an expected end.

Understanding, illumination, or revelation of a scripture at a spiritual level in a way that only the Holy Spirit can bring, is the key to receiving any of the promises of God. It is that moment when the Holy Spirit shows you the profound truth behind a scripture. It isn't enough to know the scripture or be able to quote it, you must study or meditate on it until He illuminates by His spirit the understanding of it to you.

I continued to study healing and the healing scriptures, pressing in for more knowledge, and to show myself approved so I would qualify to receive the revelations the Lord wanted to give me to share.

When you get the understanding, the scripture suddenly springs to life inside you – you suddenly "get it," or it may seem to illuminate or jump off the page of the Word to you, and He shows you what it truly means. Once you have understanding of a particular scripture or promise, you can truly claim the promise of that scripture and your faith will be released to receive from it.

This is the difference between confessing and claiming. Confessing is just repeating a scripture out loud over and over, based on a sermon you heard or a book you read. Claiming is based on *knowing* at a spiritual level that something is already yours. It is making a claim on that promise for yourself.

Understanding activates your faith in a particular promise of God. **When your confession turns to claiming, your faith is released and the promise comes to pass. Understanding was what I needed to reach my healing.**

Years earlier, I was trying to understand why my confessions were not bringing me what all the popular sermons said I could have by them. I was in a financial wilderness, and in a desperate place when the Lord taught me a very important truth.

It was early 2002, and I needed provision. I had no income, no savings, and no rent money. I prayed often and hard, my mind filled with fearful images of cut-off notices and eviction papers. During one of my prayer times, the Lord spoke.

You are already familiar with your circumstances. Stop studying your mess and look into My Word and see what I have provided for you as a way out!

So I began studying the Word more. I have always loved Ephesians 3:20, where the Word talks about God doing exceedingly, abundantly above and beyond anything we can ask or think, according to the power that works in us, but I didn't see anything above and beyond going on in my circumstances, so I decided to ask Him about it.

Ephesians 3:20
Now unto him that is able to do exceeding abundantly above all that we ask or think, according to the power that worketh in us,

Lord, what does 'according to the power that works in us' in that scripture mean?

The power that works in you will be equivalent to the depth of understanding you have of the promise in My Word you are standing on.

My understanding had been as shallow then about provision as it was now about healing. I knew more than anything else, I needed understanding. I was reminded of a verse of scripture in Proverbs.

Proverbs 4:7
Wisdom is the principal thing; therefore get wisdom: and with all thy getting get understanding.

We don't need just knowledge of what scripture says, or even wisdom. We need real revelation. We need understanding. Understanding was what tied it all together and made it work. Not understanding in our hearts, but that knowing that comes in our spirits when we truly know God has shown us one of His promises.

With understanding (revelation – the Word of God revealed to you), the Word of God takes root in your spirit and begins to produce results. Without it, you may have only frustration trying to stand on the promises.

It's not that the promises aren't good, they are absolutely true. It's that the unbelief inside you isn't in agreement with them. Without your faith being released each time you speak them, there is nothing to activate them into your circumstances. It's like having a seed, but nothing to water it with.

Proverbs 4:20-22

20 My son, attend to my words; incline thine ear unto my sayings.

21 Let them not depart from thine eyes; keep them in the midst of thine heart.

22 For they are life unto those that find them, and health to all their flesh.

Psalm 34:19

19 Many are the afflictions of the righteous: but the Lord delivereth him out of them all.

Soteria - Greek 4991 (salvation) means to rescue or safety, deliver, save, HEALTH - and if it means health, it covers healing.

I knew that the Greek word for salvation also included health, so that was another place that said my healing was included in Jesus' work at the Cross.

Every promise of God involves confessing with our mouth in order to claim it - even salvation. The Israelites had to drive out the giants - our sickness and pain or disease are like giants to us. Our bodies were created never to die, but because sin entered in, they do.

It is most helpful if you can get hold of the healing revelation while you are just dealing with something small like a headache, instead of waiting until you have a life-threatening diagnosis. Start small and experience the power of God's Word in action. Before long, you will not tolerate symptoms of sickness or pain in your body.

It is much more difficult to concentrate on the healing promises when you are wondering if you are going to be around to receive any of them.

Healing is part of the atonement which means **if you are saved, you are also entitled to be well.** We need to understand it is our right and it is God's will. Step two - all the promises of God involve confession.

Sickness and disease may be a fact; maybe the doctor told you that tests show you have whatever condition, but those are FACTS - Gods word is TRUTH - Truth will override fact and make the fact of no effect. Its like the difference in holding a Jack and an Ace in a card game. God's TRUTH is the Ace, no matter what the situation.

Fear knocked at the door. Faith answered. No one was there.

- English Proverb

Any time we hear bad news in a doctor's office, fear will try its best to overtake us, but if we have been taking in the truth of God's Word each day, our faith will answer the door for us and His Truth will override whatever we have heard that day.

If we stand on the truth of His Word, this glorifies Him. Healing manifests and displays His mighty power, plus if we're ill and in pain, we aren't going to be productive for the Kingdom. We will not feel like going into all the world.

Prov. 15:4 - A wholesome tongue is a tree of life: but perverseness therein is a breach in the spirit.

A breach is a fracture or broken place – it's like a fence broken down in your spirit. Fences keep undesirable things out. If someone *breaches* your fence, they have access to whatever is nearest the breached place. **Our negative words give the enemy access over whatever area of our lives we're speaking over.**

Our negative words create a breach in our hedge of healing, against ill health. They swing a wide gate open to the devil and all his devices to work against us in whatever area we speak of.

Proverbs 12:18

There is that speaketh like the piercings of a sword: but the tongue of the wise is health.

Years ago, I had an elderly friend that I visited almost every day. My friend suffered a lot of pain in her body and I often prayed for her.

One night as I was praying for her, the Lord spoke to me - He told me He *wanted* to heal her, but **He said every time she spoke her misery, she *established* it.**

That means every time I speak my misery, I establish my misery, and every time you speak your misery, *you establish your misery.*

Job. 22:28

Thou shalt also decree a thing, and it shall be established unto thee: and the light shall shine upon thy ways.

We must not allow our words to be stout (strong) *against* the Lord.

Malachi 3:13

Your words have been stout against me, saith the Lord. Yet ye say,

What have we spoken so much against thee?

So clearly, we must get control of our words. We want to speak health, not sickness or pain. That is really hard when we're miserable, but **every time we speak our pain and misery, we help the enemy establish it.** If we speak it 10 times a day, we made it 10 times stronger that day, and made a place for the enemy to occupy. We are letting him use our tongue to literally *help* him make us ill!

Ephesians 4:27: Neither give place to the devil.

Controlling your tongue takes a major amount of effort. When we are uncomfortable, we want to verbalize it, but verbalizing will prevent our healing. The rule is, nothing should come out of your mouth except that which you want to see happen. We get what we say, for good or ill. It's our choice what we say.

Mark 11:23

23 For verily I say unto you, That whosoever shall say unto this mountain, Be thou removed, and be thou cast into the sea; and shall not doubt in his heart, but shall believe that those things which he saith shall come to pass; he shall have whatsoever he saith.

Whenever a doctor prescribes medicine for us, we are instructed to take it a certain number of times each day. We need to speak God's Word and apply it like medicine, too. You can't speak God's Word once and speak your pain five times and think your pain will stop, it won't. **It's not what you do once in awhile that counts, it's what you do consistently - all day, every day.** If you exercise once a month, you won't see results, if you exercise once a day, you will. If I eat sugar twice a month, I probably won't see any results. If I eat it twice a day, I will most definitely see the results of it.

We need to drive out our health giants – the pain, sickness, and disease, by applying the light of His Word onto the darkness that has taken up residence in us. Every time we apply the Word, we are weakening the enemy's hold a little more.

Remember: **There was not once a time of miracles, we serve the GOD of Miracles. His miracle power never stopped, people just stopped believing.**

The Lord told me to study those who had gone before and mastered healing, and Dodie Osteen was the first one to come to my mind. Reading her small book, "Healed of Cancer," over and over a few years before was when I had first begun to get a revelation that healing was my right.

Unfortunately, that was the same time period my sister fell ill and was life-flighted to the hospital as we feared for her life, and while traveling 100% of the time with my job, I fell so ill I ended up in the emergency room twice in one weekend, following on the heels of my ex-husband's death, the father of my children.

With so much happening, and all the traveling back and forth to see everyone who needed me, I soon had my hands full just trying to get well again, and I stopped studying healing, and in turn allowed the beginning of my belief for healing to be choked out.

The enemy has many weapons in his arsenal to keep you ill.

When you're in a lot of pain or you're really sick or you've just gotten a terrible diagnosis, the enemy will try to move in on you with every lie he has to try to get you to just accept the diagnosis because he knows if you fight it, you can win. He'll tell you the sickness runs in your family, it's natural, you shouldn't try to fight it, God gave it to you for His glory, blah, blah, blah....these are all lies - sickness does *not* glorify God - we need to FIGHT IT and FIGHT IT HARD!

Once you win the healing battle once, you can walk in it from then on. The first symptom that gets on you after that, you can defeat it right away, keeping illness from even taking root.

LONG STANDING ILLNESS

In studying healing and writing this book, I could clearly see that when the enemy first begins to put symptoms on us, we have the opportunity to resist and refuse those symptoms. But what about long standing illnesses, illnesses or pains that were accepted long before we knew the truth? So I inquired of the Lord about long standing illnesses.

What about long-standing illnesses, Lord, that already have a head start on us? Or what if we caused the illness ourselves by sinning, like with drug use?

The Lord showed me that the understanding that comes through revelation in His Word is so powerful, it can actually erase the unbelief that allowed the pain, symptoms and illness to set up the stronghold in the first place. I knew I had a stronghold to tear down where my spinal problems were concerned, as they had first begun flaring up over thirty years earlier. Every time I felt pain, I would remind myself that those symptoms were just long-standing lies from the enemy of my soul who did not want to see my precious Lord glorified by healing in my body.

HEALED OF CHRONIC BACK PAIN

It is May 2019 as I update this book and I am happy to report, I seldom ever have *any* back pain now – after decades of horrible, debilitating pain sometimes every day for months on end and hundreds of chiropractic visits over the years. Fighting the healing battle detailed in this book was well worth the effort! I have not had any surgeries or done anything other than what I detailed in this book to achieve these results in my back.

SIN INDUCED ILLNESS AND DISEASE

I also remembered when I was studying healing once before in 2001, and trying to understand if we were entitled to it. I never did get the revelation back then, but one night, I asked the Lord about sin-induced illness and disease.

Lord, what if someone has a disease brought on by sin, like intravenous drug use?

If they repent and turn from their sin, I will still heal them.

What a merciful God we serve!

It may be true that you've never won the battle over pain, sickness and disease before, but you didn't know then what you know now. You have new weapons and they are the weapons that will stop the enemy, and the illness and pain, dead in their tracks.

No matter what sickness or pain the enemy brings on you, it is still one that Jesus paid for when He received those lashings before going to the cross and to accept it as your fate is to deny the power in His Blood and what He purchased for you.

Every single pain, sickness and disease was nailed to that Cross with our Lord. It was crucified when He was and we should not stand for it in our bodies. No pain, sickness or disease the enemy brings should be acceptable to us as children of the Most High God. We have been given power over *all* the power of the enemy.

That means **_all_**.

Luke 10:19

Behold, I give unto you power to tread on serpents and scorpions, and over all the power of the enemy: and nothing shall by any means hurt you.

Notice that verse says He gave **us** power over all the power of the enemy. He didn't keep it and say ask Him to handle the battle for you, He said I give unto **you** power.....that means He left us the weapons and the authority because *He wants us to fight the enemy*. This is why begging God to heal us does not work – He wants us to have a higher revelation – not only that He *can* heal us, but that we are *already healed*. If He healed us every time we begged endlessly, we would never get to the blessing of knowing we already have what we're asking Him for.

For years, I prayed and begged God to heal my back and take away my pain, not realizing He had already done His part. *And* He had already told me about it in His Word!

Satan would never cease to put pain and sickness on every part of us if he could get away with it. In some cases he does. He is the original bully. He knows it is not his right, but like any other bully, he will keep doing it until you stand up with authority and make him stop. He continually seeks even the tiniest crack in a believer's life he can work his evil and destruction into.

Accepting a pain or illness because we believe it is our fate to have that one is the equivalent of letting the neighborhood bully beat you up because you feel like you should get a beating. It is up to you to tell him you won't stand for it, to refuse it, and to fight it at every turn. We, as children of the Most High God, as the redeemed whose healing has been purchased by our precious Lord and Savior with His own blood, must stand up and tell the enemy that *no* illness, *no* pain, *no* disease is acceptable to us!

I grew up in remote rural areas of Northeast Texas. In very remote areas, you burn your refuse or carry it to the dump. Sometimes people would load up their refuse and drive around looking for a place they could dump it while no one was looking. The person being dumped on didn't know until they found the garbage piled on their land. They then had to deal with garbage that wasn't theirs.

It wasn't fair to the one who owned the land that was dumped on, but as long as no one stands up in their authority over their land, the garbage dumping will continue. It continues to this day.

Sometimes after people found truckloads of garbage dumped on their land, they began posting signs that said "No Dumping Allowed. Violators will be Prosecuted." They were serving notice on the dumpers that dumping would no longer be tolerated. In effect, they were saying, "That's your garbage, *not mine*, and you're not leaving it on my land!"

Satan is sneaky. He will keep trying to dump garbage on you that isn't yours. You've already been healed. It is up to you to stop the devil's work in your life and in your body. Jesus already did His part.

When you understand that healing truly is yours under the work Jesus did at the cross, you will start serving notice on Satan that you won't take any more. Every time you quote what the Word of God says about you being healed, you are posting a sign to Satan that says No Dumping Allowed!

In the quest for your total healing, it can help to understand how your sickness or disease manifested.

One night, I was listening to healing scriptures and meditating on healing. I had been trying to get to my healing for weeks, without any real understanding what to do, only why it was mine.

I had finally gotten the revelation that healing was something Jesus purchased at the cross for me. I studied it out and saw that it clearly is a right that belongs to every saved person, so I was confident I was entitled to healing as a Biblical covenant right and part of what He wanted me to have.

It is important to note something here. **If you have not examined the healing scriptures to the point you know for sure you are entitled to it - know as in *really* know, no book about healing is going to help you see your healing.**

I cannot emphasize this enough. We must have our own personal revelation that *our* healing was purchased at the cross. Not our fellow church goers, not just our neighbor's, but *ours* - yours and mine. Someone may pray for your healing with their faith, but you can lose it as quickly as you received it. But once you have revelation, good health is yours forever!

As I update this book in 2019, I can tell you I have enjoyed better health since getting that revelation and fighting my healing battle than ever before in my life and I will be 60 years old next year!

Until you have that, the rest of what is in this book will not help you much. I read scores of books on healing with healing scripture references and still didn't get it. Until I got alone with what the Word of God said about healing for myself, I didn't see any results coming to pass.

All that is well and good, but how did a person get it? I had read book after book on healing, using a process of elimination system, while studying the scriptures at the same time. I knew if I was entitled to it, I could have it, I just had to figure out the receiving part.

Do I just say I receive healing and then it shows up? Because I had tried that a number of times and stayed sick and in pain. Did I go around confessing by His stripes I am healed? Because I had done that, too, and so far that had not worked either. I was open to the possibility that I had not done that long enough, so that one was still on my list of things to try.

On this night, I was laying quietly on my bed to relieve the terrible fatigue that came with being in so much pain the entire day and trying to work besides.

Constant pain drains you of your energy, as well as your joy. It steals away your productivity, while draining any happiness out of your day that it can, by screaming louder than anything else in your mind. On this day, that had happened. I had gotten up feeling like I had the flu, and the pain in my arm had been strong. The muscle spasms had been continual throughout the day and I had taken a steady stream of over-the-counter pain relievers, used capsaicin cream all day long, and even visited a doctor in a nearby town to begin the diagnosis process. Nothing had really helped, other than the over-the-counter painkillers had dulled the pain enough I could function through my day. I just couldn't enjoy any of it.

The night before, I had decided to make a personal scripture recording. My friend John Morgan who was walking in his healing, had sent me his view on it, and I had come up with a list of the scriptures that spoke the loudest to me. I made a recording reading the scriptures, and also the healing viewpoints I had found in my studies to help me remember them.

One of the things that will make the most difference in your healing journey is to find scriptures that speak to *your* spirit. One scripture may speak loud to me, another to you. Your healing will manifest more quickly if you listen to and confess the ones that witness to you the most of God's mighty healing power.

The night before, I had slept with my recording playing. I had left it playing all day that day in the background, even though I could not hear it from where I work during the day. As I lay there, listening quietly to my healing recordings and meditating on those truths that night, something powerful rose up in my spirit and I began to see healing in a new way. I knew this was the revelation I had been waiting for.

I knew then the devil's days of making me ill were numbered, and I planned to make that number as small as possible.

What I saw that night is that healing is not something we need to "receive." You don't need to receive something you already have, you just need to know you have it. John Morgan had tried to teach me that many years before, but I had never gotten it.

Okay, Lord, so I have it. Where is it then?

It's there, buried under your doubt and unbelief.

I already had it!

The Lord was saying that the sins of doubt and unbelief (also caused by lack of knowledge of His Word), were what had allowed sickness and disease to manifest in my body!

Hosea 4:6

My people are destroyed for lack of knowledge: because thou hast rejected knowledge, I will also reject thee, that thou shalt be no priest to me: seeing thou hast forgotten the law of thy God, I will also forget thy children.

Unbelief is sin. To not believe what God's Word says is sin, plain and simple, so we had better know and understand what it says. We handle sin by repenting and turning from it. Something in my body had clearly exalted itself against the knowledge of God (because God says I have already been healed - that makes sickness and disease a **LIE** that exalted itself, and me in sin because I had believed the lie over the truth of His Word).

Okay, I had no problem repenting and turning from the lie of doubt and unbelief that I was healed. But how did I get the sickness to leave?

Then I saw it!

I had to establish the truth of God's Word in the place where the lie was, and use the light of the truth of His Word to drive out the darkness which was the lie of sickness and disease!

Healing was already present in His Word, but it couldn't manifest in my body, because *something else was there in the way.*

I wasn't in receive mode, I was in tearing down and rebuilding mode! That meant that every symptom I had been suffering in my body or had ever suffered, was based on a lie from the enemy. That meant every thought I had in regard to a symptom was also a lie, and it was arrogantly exalting itself against the truth of God's Word which declares I am already healed. Just as God had tried to show me years before, I needed to stop believing my symptoms and start believing my God!

II Corinthians 10:4-5

(For the weapons of our warfare are not carnal, but mighty through God to the pulling down of strong holds;)

Casting down imaginations, and every high thing that exalteth itself against the knowledge of God, and bringing into captivity every thought to the obedience of Christ;

Suddenly, I remembered what the Lord had spoken to me around the beginning of 2001 when I had injured my back doing a simple exercise. A huge purple lump had appeared on one side of my spine where the injury was, and many times during that week, I was unable to walk and literally had to crawl to get to other rooms because my spine would not support me.

Please help me, Lord! This pain is awful, and I have no money for a doctor!

Who are you going to believe - Me or your pain?

At that time, I was in a horrible financial and emotional wilderness, and my faith was not strong enough to believe Him, and I had believed the excruciating pain instead.

Consequently, I still had a weakness in that part of my spine. There were countless times I wished I had realized the revelation He was trying to get me to then and pressed in for it, but it was easier to believe the intense pain, lay back down, and beg for healing. That healing never came, because we don't get healing by begging for it. If we did, I would have been healed long before my latest run-in with pain and sickness.

Believing in sickness and disease creates a stronghold in our minds. Hearing the doctor's reports over and over and studying our disease to see what will happen next adds to that stronghold - a lot. Expectation of the next symptom leads to us putting our faith in those symptoms and the power of the disease instead of in the power of our mighty God.

The pain and other symptoms reinforce the stronghold, making it seem true. It becomes easier to believe our pain and symptoms that are right there with us than the glorious truth that Jesus took a horrible lashing to purchase our complete healing - mind, body and spirit, if only we will fight the enemy for it.

Many people who suffer severe symptoms of disease think so much on their disease that it becomes all they can talk about. When this happens, the disease has become their identity, and no illness should ever be our identity. Our identity is as a Child of God.

Tearing down a stronghold is a major fight, but it is not an impossible fight. A stronghold of lies is hacked down using the sword of truth - the Word of God.

Several years earlier, I was praying one night when the Lord showed me a vision I call the Sword of the Word. I saw a beautiful sword and its blade was cut up in sections like jigsaw puzzle pieces. One or two pieces were missing. The base of the sword had the word salvation on it. I saw other foundational truths on other pieces. The Healing piece was not there. The Lord showed me that I had nothing to fight with in some areas of my life in that vision. I knew healing was one of those areas.

If you are gearing up for war, where do you attack the hardest? Where your enemy is the weakest. Satan knows whether we have revelation about healing or not.

I had already begun sharpening my sword, gearing up for battle with the enemy.

I now knew that tearing down the stronghold of lies the enemy had sold me would be the toughest part of the battle. That stronghold had a fifty-two year head start on me, but I was determined it was going to fall, and fall hard.

Romans 4:19-20

And being not weak in faith, he considered not his own body now dead, when he was about an hundred years old, neither yet the deadness of Sarah's womb: He staggered not at the promise of God through unbelief; but was strong in faith, giving glory to God;

Remember Abraham - then Abram. He listened only to the words of His God about the child of promise. He didn't listen to any opposing doctor's reports, anything any well-meaning acquaintances trying to give him a "reality check" said, he listened only to the words of his mighty God, and he meditated on those. **What he waited for didn't happen right away. He had lots of chances to give up, but he never did.** He just kept on believing.

He knew God was faithful. It was twenty-five years before the promise was fulfilled to Abraham and Sarah, but God was faithful to His Word. And He is still faithful to His Word today.

Abraham received the fulfillment of the promise because he refused to consider or believe anything except God's Word to him. You and I receive the fulfillment of our promises exactly the same way.

God's Word declared me healed, so it didn't matter what anyone else said. His Word was the final authority in my life and I would continue to stand on it until I saw my full healing manifest, however long that took. I knew the only other option was to accept the pain and illness, and bow down to the enemy's attack on my body.

Unless you have the truth of the first two steps in your spirit, don't proceed to step three. You will only set yourself up for attack – and failure - if you do.

If you do have revelation - true revelation - in your spirit, that healing is your absolute right, be prepared to do battle for however long you must and be aware the enemy is going to do his utmost to make you doubt or back down from your stand so you won't be able to drive out his lies. He will try to hit you with new attacks, to see if he can land one on you that you find 'acceptable.' Maybe one that runs in your family?

Just remember, those stripes Jesus took for us covered **all** sickness and disease. All means ALL.

Are you ready for a fight? You will have to fight to tear down the lies and unbelief that have caused sickness, pain and disease to affect your body, but once you get this, sickness and disease will never have power over you again!

Haven't you waited long enough to make healing yours?

As the pain lessened slightly later that afternoon, I quickly attempted to do all my necessary tasks. The last task on my list was to shower and wash my waist length hair. As I pressed the clip to let my long hair down in preparation, I felt the pain trying to return to my shoulders. Muscle spasms took over one of my arms and the pain of raising it announced its return as my hair tumbled down in loose waves over my shoulders.

I stopped and looked at my arm, seeing the muscles tightening into spasms, as my jaw clenched at the intense pain shooting through it. Twice earlier in the day, I had confessed my list of scriptures out loud, claiming my complete healing in every area, praising God I was already healed, and rejoicing that I would soon see it manifested in every part of my body. And I meant it, too.

I knew healing was mine, and if healing was mine, that meant those symptoms of pain and muscle spasms *weren't*.

Righteous anger rose up in me as a sharp stabbing pain shot through my left arm again, and Isaiah 53:5 began pouring out of me. I began warring in tongues and commanding the pain to leave in the Name of Jesus. It stopped in that part of my arm and moved down.

I rebuked it again and commanded it to leave, quoting Isaiah 53:5 over and over, declaring my healing and telling my arm it was healed. The pain moved again. It went further down my arm.

Oh no he didn't!

The enemy was moving the pain around!

Suddenly, I saw in my spirit **he was moving it to see if I would *accept it* if it afflicted some other area!**

Righteous fury rose up in me. He was about to find out that I could be relentless when it came to pain that stopped me from writing!

When I saw what he was doing, I kicked into full warfare mode. He was **not** going to do this to me.

Righteous anger fueled me on as I thought about having to arrange my schedule around the pain and immobility he had put on me, when it wasn't even mine. As I increased the intensity of my warfare, the pain stopped. It moved further down, this time all the way into my hand.

*No he **didn't***!

Yes, he *did*! He still thought I would accept the pain if he found the right place! The pain in my hand increased. I refused to relent. He was **not** going to do this to me. Jesus had paid for my healing and it was mine, and I was going to have it!

After warring a few more minutes and rebuking the pain over and over, it finally left, and did not return for hours. In fact, I had more use of my arms than I had had in days. Later that night, it tried to return, and I rebuked it again.

I was learning as I went, and it was starting to look like a lot of my healing manifestation would be linked to warring against the enemy and demanding he remove the symptoms he was trying to put on me.

Whatever was causing the pain in my arms and other parts of my body, none of it had the right to be there based on the fact that Jesus had purchased my healing. Period.

As far as I was concerned, I would war every day for the rest of my life if that was what it took to overcome, but I was determined the enemy would *not* put anything on me Jesus had paid to remove!

The next day, I had very little pain in either shoulder, and every time pain did try to come, I immediately rebuked it and I spoke to my shoulders and arms that they were healed by the stripes of Jesus, until it receded.

Mark 7:31-35

31 And again, departing from the coasts of Tyre and Sidon, he came unto the sea of Galilee, through the midst of the coasts of Decapolis.

32 And they bring unto him one that was deaf, and had an impediment in his speech; and they beseech him to put his hand upon him.

33 And he took him aside from the multitude, and put his fingers into his ears, and he spit, and touched his tongue;

34 And looking up to heaven, he sighed, and saith unto him, Ephphatha, that is, Be opened.

35 And straightway his ears were opened, and the string of his tongue was loosed, and he spake plain.

It is important to note that **in this accounting of one of the miracles Jesus performed, He spoke to the body part that wasn't lining up "Be opened."** I saw the most healing manifest in my body after I received revelation, when I spoke to the actual body part that was ill or hurting and told it that it was healed by the stripes of Jesus.

That night, I felt misery try to take over my body and my strength leave as a familiar illness began manifesting itself. For years, every spring I had suffered at least one terrible respiratory infection that lasted for weeks. I always attributed it to the pollens of all that bloomed and blew in the breeze because the first one usually showed up around the same time. Some years when my body was especially run down, I had suffered many. In 2006, I had been stricken six or seven times, and at least three times in 2007 while traveling with my job. I spent hundreds of dollars on medicines and sometimes antibiotics as it progressed to get through each one, and it was not uncommon for it to last ten days at a time.

When I felt the familiar, flu-like symptoms beginning, I realized the enemy had begun another attack in a different way, again to see if I would accept illness in a different form.

Anyone who has ever suffered from recurrent viruses or infections knows that familiar misery you feel when one begins to affect your body. All you really want to do is go to bed and pull the covers over your head until it's gone. I knew this time a virus was attacking me, and I knew if it became full-blown, I would be more or less shut down for two weeks trying to heal from it. I didn't have two weeks to throw away and not only that, I was angry the enemy was attempting to make me miserable yet again. I went after him with a vengeance.

I had never beat a respiratory infection, but I had never really warred against one before, not having the full revelation that healing was mine. This time I did. I warred in tongues and in English and told the enemy he would **not** put that illness on me, that I was already healed, and I quoted the scriptures that said so. I also spoke to my body and told it that it was healed in the Name of Jesus and I commanded it to line up with the Word of God. I commanded it to obey in the Name of Jesus.

The virus left. Within hours I could feel no trace of it at all. **God truly watches over His Word to perform it if we will only speak it out of our mouths with faith and stand in our authority as believers!**

It is an awesome feeling to win a battle like this against the enemy, especially when he has put something like that on you so many times before and gotten away with it. I truly wished I had studied healing years earlier, instead of just taking whatever the enemy afflicted me with.

As you pursue your complete healing, it is important to realize the enemy knows what illnesses you have accepted before, and which you expect to get because of your genetics. He has heard every conversation you've had and seen every article you have read. He also knows your fears, because he gave them to you.

Even though we accepted pretty much whatever he brought on us in the past, he will try them all again in an attempt to find one we find "acceptable." In other words, one we think we are supposed to have or can do nothing about because we always get it, because everyone in our family has had it, because it's going around, because it's common for our age group, or just because we've never won the battle over it before.

He has studied you long enough to know how you look at whatever illnesses are common for your age and genetics, and what you feel is an "acceptable" level of pain or illness, or even debilitation as you age, what you believe "runs in your family," and what illness or pain you have told others you will likely end up with. **Sickness and disease are part of the curse and you don't have to tolerate them if you are a child of the Most High God and walking with Him. The enemy knows you don't have to tolerate it, but he also knows whether *you* know it or not.**

He knows whether you truly have revelation on healing or not, and until you do, you will always be open to attacks on your body from him.

The Lord told me at the very beginning of my healing journey that I could approach healing boldly, because He had already healed me.

He has already healed you, too. He has already healed all of us who are saved. And the clock in heaven always says "NOW."

I Peter 2:24 says by His stripes we *were* healed - past tense – which means it has *already happened*.

For us the work comes in taking what has already been done or given to us. **Since we cannot see the healing work, and we *can* see the symptoms of sickness, in the natural we will accept the symptoms far more easily.** They're easier to see, right? So they are easier to believe. That's why this is where the fight is.

Some pastors teach that sickness is the will of God, that God gets glory from it. Really? Then why did Jesus go around pulling sickness off of people and not putting it on them? He was here to glorify God. If sickness would bring His Father glory, He would have been putting it out all over the place.

But He didn't. He did just the opposite. Over and over, scripture tells us, He healed all who came to Him.

All of them. That means if you had been among the sick in the days of Jesus, He would have healed you, not turned you away while He healed everyone else. And He is still the same today – He wants to heal *you*.

He didn't say to one, Okay, you get to be healed today, and to another, Oh, wait, it's My Father's will for *you* to be sick. You poor thing, you're going to bring Him so much glory laying in your bed suffering like that for Him.

Glory? How on earth can sickness be glorifying? Jesus already suffered for our sickness when He took that horrible scourging to glorify God. That's the equivalent of saying His sacrifice wasn't enough and that it needs our help.

The only way us suffering glorifies God is when we suffer by laying down sins we enjoy, or when we sacrifice comfort to minister to others, those kinds of things. Sickness never glorifies God.

Hearing teaching that God puts sickness on us for His glory, or that it is sometimes His will can convince you to accept sickness as your lot in life, but think about it. How could your sickness or disease possibly glorify God unless He heals you of it and gives you a testimony? That is the only way it could bring Him glory. **Sickness does not bring glory. It brings a lot of things, but glory isn't one of them.** It brings pain, debilitation and medical bills, but not glory. And who would want to serve a God who makes His own people sick?

You must understand that God wants you to be well. That's why He put I Peter 2:24 in His Word, He wants you to know He has already provided that for you so you don't have to be sick one day in your life.

Some denominations teach that miracles stopped with the Apostles, and this is also clearly not true. In Acts Chapter 9, someone clearly not one of the Apostles was sent to lay hands on Saul of Tarsus that he might receive his sight back.

There were also all the disciples Christ sent out in twos (the seventy) who went about healing and casting out evil spirits. These were obviously not just the original twelve.

After the resurrection of Christ, miracles continued to happen within the early church and they continue to happen today. Denominational teaching that miracles, healings and other spiritual gifts stopped after the Apostles always make me think of 2 Timothy 3:5:

2 Timothy 3:5

Having a form of godliness, but denying the power thereof: from such turn away.

They look godly, they sound godly, but demonstrate none of His power. There are no signs and wonders following, which makes us ask the question of whether there is any belief.

Mark 16:17-18

17 And these signs shall follow them that believe; In my name shall they cast out devils; they shall speak with new tongues;

18 They shall take up serpents; and if they drink any deadly thing, it shall not hurt them; they shall lay hands on the sick, and they shall recover.

The Lord wants His power flowing through His children and His church. Those teaching that miracles and healings have stopped should be prayed for, not condemned. Somewhere along the way, they have just received wrong teaching themselves, and the enemy is holding them in deception. But we should not listen to those wrong beliefs.

By mid-May, I had been struggling to discipline myself to exercise every day in spite of the pain in my shoulders, and had begun walking on my treadmill and occasionally bicycling in an effort to shed the thirty extra pounds I felt I had carried around for years. I was seeing results and was really encouraged.

One evening while walking on my treadmill, my foot slipped and the treadmill threw me into the wooden shelf next to it. The next morning, I had a dark purple bruise on my hip to show for it. I had oiled the treadmill just a few days before and some of the oil always came up on the edges of the belt. I deduced that I must have stepped onto the oil and slipped.

A few days later, I woke up in terrible pain, pain so bad that every movement hurt. It felt as if someone had driven a dagger into one of my shoulder blades. I was worn out from fighting the enemy on so many fronts at once, I made an appointment with the chiropractor and prayed hard for relief. I had battled through many pains and illnesses, but I did not know how to fight through pain so bad I could hardly breathe.

Even the five-minute drive to my chiropractor's office was torture. When your spine is injured and becomes inflamed, even the slightest movement causes excruciating pain.

That night, with the pain screaming even after having an adjustment and using an ice pack, I dug around in my medicine chest and found a few pain pills left over from a bout of sciatica. I hate taking painkillers, especially prescription ones, but I was desperate for relief, and for some rest from the pain. I took one and as I waited for it to take effect, the Lord spoke to me.

Until you fight the enemy and receive your healing, he will continue putting more pain and sickness on you. He will keep increasing it until you get healed and write the book.

I hadn't been praying when the Lord spoke, but what He said reinforced what He had told me when my shoulder had first begun hurting. I would have to fight this time, and fight hard.

That night, though, the pain was so bad, there wasn't any fight in me. On top of that, I had gotten busy with other things, and I had stopped really pressing in to learn more about healing, the same thing that had happened all the other times. I knew for sure it was mine, and I quoted the scriptures every day. Why wasn't that enough? I wished there was an easier way!

Now, here I was, having to rely on pain medication to get me through. As usual, I had so many irons in the fire that I didn't know which one to deal with first, but it was clear healing would become my number one priority if this pain continued. The pain had stopped me from doing anything that day other than praying. I couldn't afford to just shut down like that. I didn't know anyone who could. I needed to receive the manifestation of my healing and receive it quick.

Okay, Lord. I'll try to do better. But tonight, there just isn't any fight in me!

I have never liked pain pills. Most of the time they made me feel more sick than anything else. When it kicked it, it finally stopped the pain in my shoulder blade that felt like someone was stabbing me, and I was left with just a needle-like burning pain in my mid-spine, so I went to bed.

The problem was, I could only lie flat on my back, and three hours later, sleep still evaded me. I was lying in bed staring at the ceiling, so I meditated on why I had not been able to move forward in my healing.

One of the problems with tearing down the lies and unbelief planted in our minds by the enemy is that **when we read healing books that tell us to confess God's Word about healing and we confess it over and over and don't see our symptoms leave, our human tendency is to say that God failed us. But God *never* fails.** It isn't even possible for Him to fail. What failed was *us*. Here's why.

To receive any of the promises in the Bible, we must claim them by faith. How do we release our faith so we can receive? By speaking. We speak the promises by faith. ***The problem comes when our speaking has no faith behind it.***

If we have not been diligent to study the healing scriptures for ourselves and find where we are entitled to healing with our own eyes, we are trying to get healed on someone else's faith and that never works. You must get the healing revelation for yourself. If you have no real understanding - the kind that comes when God illuminates those scriptures to *you*, then you are just parroting the scriptures - repeating what you've been told, *with no real Bible faith behind your words.*

Over the next several days, I continued the same method of confessing.

In my mind, I no longer saw myself as sick needing to get well, I saw myself as healed and the enemy trying to put sickness on me.

This is a very crucial element of receiving the manifestation of your healing. You must understand at the spiritual level that *He already healed you.* When you get the revelation that you are already healed, this is how you will see yourself – healed.

Whenever the pain would try to return, I would attack it with the Word of God, repeating my confessions several times and speaking to the body part that hurt and applying Isaiah 53:4 to it and commanding it to be healed and line up with the Word of God in the Name of Jesus.

I spoke the scriptures out loud with boldness and continued to repeat them over and over until the pain receded. I noticed, too, that after months of my pain level increasing to almost unbearable levels at times, it continually *decreased* as I chose to believe what the Word said and attack it over and over.

Healing like this is seldom a quick process, though it sometimes happens quickly once your faith is strong in the truth that you are already healed. You have to set your face like flint that you are not going to settle for less than all Jesus died to give you, then keep hitting the problem with the hammer of the Word until Satan's plan against you shatters into dust.

Several days after I stopped taking Naproxen or any other over the counter anti-inflammatory medication, inflammation began returning to my lower spine. I knew the enemy was trying me again. I attacked the inflammation exactly the same way I had been attacking the pain. I used the same confessions, only I replaced the word 'pain' with the word 'inflammation.' I declared Isaiah 53:4 and 1 Peter 2:24 were flowing through my veins and through my spine.

I spoke to the inflammation, cursed it, and commanded it to leave my body in the Name of Jesus, then I spoke to my spine and commanded it to be healed and line up with the Word of God in Jesus' Name.

In less than half an hour, the inflammation left.

Usually a double-dose of Naproxen and an ice pack only brought minimal relief once the inflammation started up!

Remember that whatever you focus on and speak about becomes bigger. As humans, we have a tendency to talk about whatever is wrong with us. This is especially tempting when we are fearful, uncomfortable or in pain.

If you don't want that pain and illness getting bigger, don't talk about it. This includes talking about it in writing, y'all. This will require constant vigilance over your words and great self-discipline, but it is crucial to your healing.

Proverbs 12:18

There is that speaketh like the piercings of a sword: but the tongue of the wise is health.

I knew there were steps to healing and none of the steps could be skipped. I had figured that much out. I knew healing was already mine under the atonement, and since I knew the scriptures that stated that, and had been quoting those, I was at a loss to explain why my physical condition had not gotten better, but worse. I knew it was literally impossible to apply the Word of God to any situation day after day and that situation remain the same. There was far too much power in God's Word for that to happen.

As I was meditating on this, my mind went back to an earlier wilderness - a scary financial wilderness.

It was the first week of February 2002 and I was in a dire financial situation. I still had not been able to pay my rent for that month. I had been searching everywhere for work, but the job market was tight and nothing had turned up yet. I was struggling not to panic, and seeking God for answers on why I had no provision when I had been believing Him to provide for me. I was a tither and stood on the promise of the tithe. That night I prayed.

Lord, what am I doing wrong? I am where You lead me, doing Your work, writing and doing the newsletter for You, witnessing to anyone and everyone I can witness to, studying Your Word, spending time in prayer and in Your presence every single day. I don't understand why Your provision isn't here. What am I doing wrong? Please tell me!

Fruit. Thoughts.

Fruit thoughts? Lord, I know I think too much about food...

No.

Fruit. Thoughts. Faith without works is dead.

I grabbed my Bible and quickly found James 2:26.

James 2:26

For as the body without the spirit is dead, so faith without works is dead also.

Show me, Lord. What are You telling me?

Suddenly, He illuminated my spirit. I saw that my words were confessing provision, but the screen of my mind, or my imagination, was showing me lack. I constantly imagined past due bills and my utilities being cut off. I saw myself not being able to pay my rent and having nowhere to go. Those thoughts came uninvited, but still I had not cast them down either. I had allowed them to play out in my mind. **He showed me that whatever I saw on the screen of my mind was what I *truly* believed and that until that changed, my words of confession would produce nothing.**

They would produce no works, and by that show that my faith in the area of financial provision was dead.

The fact that my faith was not working was trying to tell me I had dead faith. I had thoughts of lack and those thoughts were producing the fruit of lack in my life. The fruit of my thoughts was what He wanted me to see.

Faith without works is dead, I thought. I rolled it over and over in my mind. *He's trying to tell me I have dead faith even though my words say I am believing for provision!*

The screen of my mind was the report of my spirit, and there was no faith there. All I saw was unpaid bills and scary circumstances on that screen.

As I pondered my present pain, I realized I could not see myself healed in my mind.

It was the mind screen thing again!

Our minds command our bodies. So if I can't get the picture of me healed on my mind screen, my mind can't produce the command for my body to follow. I realized then that there was no use in going any further until I could see myself healed in my mind.

The image in our mind is the "believe" part of Mark 11:23-24 that tears down the lies and unbelief sickness and pain had established!

Mark 11:23-24

For verily I say unto you, That whosoever shall say unto this mountain, Be thou removed, and be thou cast into the sea; and shall not doubt in his heart, but shall believe that those things which he saith shall come to pass; he shall have whatsoever he saith.

Therefore I say unto you, What things soever ye desire, when ye pray, believe that ye receive them, and ye shall have them.

Faith without works is dead. If your faith isn't producing fruit, then you have dead faith.

Go back a step and get some faith. When I can see it, I can have faith for it. I can't have faith for nothing - if I see nothing in my mind when I confess healing, or worse, if I still see myself sick and in pain, then my faith in the area of healing is dead. **I will have faith for being sick and in pain, but not for being healed and healthy.**

I need to "see" what it is I desire before I can receive it. I had not seen myself healthy and well in years in the natural, so I was in for a challenge on this step.

Our circumstances automatically program our faith unless we have renewed our minds in His Word. If you want to change your life in any area, you must first renew your mind in that area. If you have trouble seeing yourself healed, look at pictures of when you were healthy – do it daily. And pray for His help with seeing your healing – your *complete* healing – don't settle for less than Jesus died to give you!

Romans 12:2

And be not conformed to this world: but be ye transformed by the renewing of your mind, that ye may prove what is that good, and acceptable, and perfect, will of God.

Until the screen of your mind shows you the new image, it won't matter what else you do. The picture on your mind screen is telling you your belief does not match the words you are saying.

The beautiful part of this is, the Word of God is so powerful, that if you continue meditating on it long enough, it will reprogram your mind and begin to show you a new image on your mind screen. It is like water and the more you encounter it, the more it sinks in.

This takes longer for some than for others, and I think much of that depends on how long you have seen yourself sick, and how many people around you are telling you how sick you are. It also depends on how much you really believe God's Word about your healing. If you really don't believe you're healed, you can say it a thousand times and feel the same. **Unbelief blocks so many of the miracles God wants us to experience.**

Your mind works just like a computer. My computer shows me what the operating system is currently capable of producing. **The picture on my monitor shows me the program currently running. Your mind screen is the same. It shows you what program is currently running in your body, Healing or Sickness.**

And whatever it is programmed to do, whatever it is showing you, is what it will ultimately produce.

I still saw myself sick and in pain. And that was exactly what I was getting.

The Lord had told me back in 2008 when I was suffering terrible pain every day, that the reason my spine was not healed was because I did not *expect* it to be healed. I had hoped for healing back then, prayed for it and begged for it. But because my faith was dead in the area of healing, I did not expect it. Now I understood even more what He had meant by that. I just had to figure out how to start expecting.

I knew I had to see myself healed before I could receive, so I began meditating on being healed and seeing myself healed and healthy in my mind at the same time. I worked at imagining myself doing all the things I had not been able to do for years because of the pain and stiffness in my lower spine.

I quickly saw that when I was in intense pain was not the best time to do the mind work, but I had so far been unable to completely stop the pain, so I kept trying. It seemed a little easier when I was sitting outside in the sunlight.

Another important factor about what we are expecting comes into play when we study our disease or illness. As humans, we don't like walking into the unknown. For example, let's say I have just been diagnosed with cancer. The doctor says there is a cancer in my body and it is growing and could eventually cause my death.

My first instinct, after fear and panic, is probably going to be to learn the progression of the disease. I want to know what's going to happen to me next. That's fine if you are going to give in to the sickness, but it is **not** conducive to fighting for your healing. The reason is because knowing about the progression creates images in your mind and those images **instruct** your body to manifest those results. Plus the enemy is going to torment you with the knowledge of what is coming once you have it. Sort of another version of the knowledge of good and evil.

Sometimes we also have family members or friends who passed away from the same diagnosis we now face. We have seen the progression. We *know* what is coming. In these cases, it is very easy for the enemy to get us into fear, and this is when we must fight even harder against the fear and also the disease. No matter what you have seen or know, no matter what *runs* in your family, it doesn't have the right to run over you! No matter how the diagnosis progresses for others, *you* are a child of the Most High God. His Truth will always override facts if we will stand on the truth and proclaim it.

Let's say I have advanced lung cancer. Let's say it's progressed to a point where the doctor knows the next place it will likely spread is to my brain. I want to be healed, but I have followed my human instinct and studied the disease that was pronounced against me. So now I know that as the disease progresses, I can expect headaches, changes in my vision and equilibrium, nausea and seizures.

Now all the enemy has to do is hit me with a bad headache and start telling me it's spread. I will receive the headache *because I am expecting* it. I know that's one of the next symptoms, so I get into fear because I buy into his lie. I start meditating on it and believing it – **so now that I am believing it, I've released my faith into it spreading to my brain and he has a legal right to put that on me**. Do you see the dangers of knowing every symptom of the progression of a serious diagnosis, and thinking about them?

How much better would it be if I didn't know and I immediately began fighting the cancer in general with God's Word? The enemy would have a much harder time getting me to buy into another symptom and hence, the progression of the disease. This is another reason it helps to have fewer people knowing what is wrong with you. Because if others know that diagnosis, you won't be the only one watching for and talking about those next symptoms, those who care for you also will, and if you have any enemies, they will, too. The last thing any of us needs is a bunch of people prophesying sickness and disease over our lives. Or worse.

That week, the pain continued to worsen in my spine as it became constant. Trying to sleep became almost a joke, there is no comfortable position when you have spinal pain in more than one area of the spine, and the pain awakened me again and again, announcing itself and refusing to be ignored. The misery at times intensified by the minute. It became common for me to be up all night in pain, or to be awakened in the wee hours of the morning, unable to sleep because the pain had come back again. It felt as if a dagger were sticking in my upper spine and hot needles in the lower spine. The pain was awful.

In between ice packs, pain patches, and whatever other over-the-counter help I could find to dull the pain, I praised God and slowly began fighting for my healing by quoting scripture after healing scripture, and declaring myself healed by the stripes of Jesus.

I knew I had to establish the truth of God's Word in my body to drive out the pain and disease. I knew it would take consistent, repeated applications of His Word in order to do that. The battle looked daunting, and there was never a time I felt less like fighting than when I hurt so badly, but the only other option was to give up and let the enemy win, and to me that was no option at all. I simply had to press in.

When the pain became its most intense, I could not concentrate on anything, but I continued doing my twice weekly radio shows and working on my writing as much as possible. If I showed the enemy he could stop me with more pain, he would only increase his attacks.

By Memorial Day Weekend, I was in a miserable state. My pain level was so high and the pain so constant day and night, that I struggled even to answer emails. Few things made any difference in its intensity. I made a few visits to the chiropractor out of desperation, but they were of little value, offering only the slightest relief, as the pain always returned within an hour, worse than before. It became clear there was only one way to get help, and that was from above. **God wanted me to find the answer in His Word alone, and He would not allow relief to come from any other**

place. He knew because of the pain, I would keep pressing in. It was for my benefit, as well as the benefit of many others. If I did not manifest my healing, I could not write the book He had instructed me to write.

The constant pain, all the over-the-counter pain relievers I was taking, and my inability to keep up my daily walking routine seemed to be further stressing my immune system. My body seemed to be weakening by the day, and I was suffering horrible fatigue from dealing with the pain and the lack of sleep.

On the Friday night before Memorial Day Weekend, my body began manifesting symptoms of an upper respiratory infection or strep throat in addition to the intense pain. I knew I would have to act and act fast, or I was going to be worse than miserable for the next couple of weeks. I could not even imagine enduring that level of constant pain *and* strep throat at the same time.

I was beginning to understand more about the mind screen and how it worked. This was clearly how the devil was getting the door open to put more sickness on us. It worked a lot like the anatomy of temptation I had just discovered in my study of weight loss and self discipline. The only difference was, the enemy was tempting me to be ill, instead of tempting me with something sweet.

So Satan tempts us to see if we will accept or not accept sickness and disease when he brings it, just like he tempted Eve with the fruit.

Satan knows every child of God has already had their healing purchased for them, but he also knows if he can get us to go along with the sickness and deny the work of the Cross, that he has the legal right to put sickness and pain on us. All he has to do is get us to accept the sickness and start putting our expectation in it, and he's got us. Our bodies will produce the spoiled fruit of pain, sickness and disease.

Because the enemy brings sickness like he brings sin, it is worth the time to look at and understand the anatomy of temptation. By understanding temptation, you can see where you are at any given time in the process of receiving or accepting something like sickness or sin.

Every person who has ever attempted to lose weight or deal with an addiction and failed knows the power of a tempting thought. As I pressed in to my weight loss journey, I began to study the anatomy of temptation.

I had read scores of books on how to lose weight and get in shape. I knew I was supposed to resist bad foods and eat good ones. We all know that, right? The goal is to learn to eat healthy foods and like them, and not want the junk foods that made us overweight and unhealthy. But let's face it. That's a lot easier said than done. If that wasn't the case, two-thirds of Americans wouldn't be overweight. There is nothing easy about reprogramming long-standing food preferences.

Reprogramming your mind not to accept illness will also be a challenge, but one you can easily overcome when you realize none of those symptoms are yours.

So I began to study how temptation happens. I wanted to understand how we are tempted, and what makes us keep doing something we know is wrong for us, or that brings the exact opposite of the result we want.

James 1:14-15 holds the key to the anatomy of temptation and how it leads to sin.

James 1:14-15

But every man is tempted, when he is drawn away of his own lust, and enticed. Then when lust hath conceived, it bringeth forth sin: and sin, when it is finished, bringeth forth death.

But every man is tempted - this is when we have the thought of the wrong thing - in this case, it is the thought of getting sick, or of a certain symptom being present and impending sickness or disease

when he is drawn away - this is when we see the imagination, or picture on our mind screen, of the illness and our future suffering with it

of his own lust - when we lust we are starting to enjoy the imaginations of doing the wrong thing, eating the wrong food or believing the illness. Where sickness and pain are concerned, we aren't lusting after it, but we are definitely entertaining the thought at an intense level by giving it so much of our attention (and often other people's attention as well). The result is the same. **We are staring at it and allowing it to program our minds. We are supposed to stare at the Word of God and let our minds be programmed by *that*.**

and enticed - as we continue to hold the imaginations in our mind and play them over and over, as we see ourselves enjoying the forbidden food or drug or sin. With illness, we see ourselves ill, in pain, even dying, until we begin believing the imaginations, and our will to resist becomes weaker and weaker - now we are in real danger of actually doing or receiving the wrong thing. The faith that produced the imaginations will fuel the manifestation in our bodies of what we see in our minds.

Then when lust hath conceived - where sin is concerned, this is where we actually yield to the sin. Where ill health is concerned, this is when the symptoms really take over everything, over all our energy and thoughts and expectations, and we are believing far more in the power of the disease and the pain than in the power of the Word to heal us.

it bringeth forth sin - the result of the conception of sin is the commission of the act of sin, or in the case of ill health, the fullness of the sickness manifesting in our bodies.

In sinful acts, the conception happens when the thought of wrongdoing and the imaginations come together. After a time, sin is conceived in the mind. **Where the mind leads, the behavior will always eventually follow if it is not stopped.**

Where illness is concerned, it is the conception of the enemy's suggestion that we are ill, and our process of entertaining it and thinking on it that allow the illness to be conceived and brought to full manifestation in our bodies.

and sin, when it is finished, bringeth forth death. - the wages of sin is always death in some area. The wages of entertaining sickness can be too, if the illness is a serious one.

Years ago, I think it was around the end of 2001, I injured my spine while working out with weights. I did a weight lifting move I didn't realize pulled on the lower back. A huge blue and purple lump swelled out on one side of my spine where I injured it. I was out of work and out of money, and I had no health insurance, so there was no way to go to a doctor. The pain was so bad I had to stay in bed, and many days I would lower myself out of the bed and crawl to the bathroom because my injured spine refused to allow me to stand up.

One night the pain was so intense, I was on my knees beside my bed weeping and begging the Lord to heal me. I knew nothing about healing then, so I thought I was supposed to ask Him for it, like I asked for everything else. He spoke this to me:

Who are you going to believe? Me or your pain?

I wanted to believe Him, but honestly, the pain was screaming much louder, and I chose to believe it instead, so I got to keep the pain and the injured spine. I answered the Lord honestly, but it was the wrong answer. He wanted me to press in and get a revelation on what He had provided for me in His Word and I was hurting too bad to do that. I lay in bed in terrible pain and begged Him to heal me instead. Many, many times over the years that followed, I desperately wished I had pursued healing back then. It would have saved me so much misery.

We are believers, not beggars.

Why are our thoughts and imaginations so powerful, Lord?

Because they program your mind.

I was immediately reminded of the lesson about the fruit of our thoughts.

Our minds are more than our thoughts. Our imaginations are like little power generators – for good or for ill, literally. **Whatever our imagination continually sees, our body develops.** Our imaginations are constantly giving commands to our bodies through the images they produce in response to words. And those words can be written or spoken.

Which means, if my imagination shows my mind images of me being sick with the flu, it is giving commands to my body to be sick with the symptoms of the flu. If my mind thinks I may have cancer, my body may start manifesting the symptoms of cancer.

The Lord showed me as I was studying healing that whenever the first symptom or thought of illness presents itself, **we need to decide whether we will get in agreement with the sickness and symptoms, or whether we will get into agreement with His Word, which declares we are already healed.**

That one decision starts the process – either of healing or of getting sicker. The choice is ours.

He already did His part.

I program my Garmin GPS device to get me where I want to go on a trip. *Get me where I'm going, Garmin.* I punch in the address of my destination, and it gives me turn-by-turn directions as I travel my route. It won't let me go anywhere but where I program it to take me. If I make a wrong turn, it 'recalculates' and gets me back on track to the destination I programmed it with. **The key to using the power of a Garmin is to program it with the right destination. The key to using the power of our minds is the same, only as Christians, we are to program our minds with the Word of God.**

As the enemy continued to try to put strep or an upper respiratory infection on me in addition to the terrible pain I was already in, I was able to identify the process and break it down into steps.

* First, he produces a symptom in your body. (like the pain and intense pain in my throat in this case, and the sick virus feeling in my body).

* The symptom is followed by a thought *"Oh no, I'm coming down with strep!"*

* An image is created in reaction to the thought and is displayed on my mind screen for me to consider - suddenly I see myself not only in terrible pain, but now also miserable from the symptoms of strep, and I see it going on for two weeks. Having to spends hundreds of dollars on the doctor and medicine. Falling behind on my work. Bedridden, in terrible pain, feverish…

* If I accept the thought that I have strep throat and begin considering or worrying over the possibilities that brings (how miserable I will be, how will I get my work done, the cost of going to the doctor for antibiotics, etc.), my emotions will also get in on the game. **Your emotions release your faith fully into the situation.**

I began to plan my strategy.

I knew receiving healing would be a fight. So far I had launched the fight only in short spurts, going back to my usual busy schedule in between, trying not to get too far behind. I was pretty sure this time I would have to press in for hours at a time, if not days and weeks, in order to see my healing begin to manifest. Starting the battle and then backing down would do little more than back the pain off for a little while and increase the enemy's attack on me. I would have to set my face like flint. It reminded me of a scripture in Isaiah.

Isaiah 50:7

For the Lord GOD will help me; therefore shall I not be confounded: therefore have I set my face like a flint, and I know that I shall not be ashamed.

I chose to spend the holiday weekend battling because I knew my daily routine would slow down as far as emails and mail to answer, and I thought it might be easier to concentrate, plus the added symptoms of sickness motivated me. I knew if I delayed the fight, that sickness would set in and likely make me too ill to act for weeks to come.

I felt my sole focus would have to be on mastering healing and I decided to start with what I knew had worked on the lesser symptoms before the pinched nerve had come along to add to my misery.

The Lord had told me to study those who had mastered healing and see what steps they had gone through, and that I would have to fight for my healing. I planned to do just that. I was sure He would reveal anything else I needed to do as I battled.

I rounded up my healing teachings and books and began putting together an abbreviated scripture list to pray. I planned to listen to healing teachings, read portions of the books, and recite the scriptures, attacking the pain and sickness over and over. I knew Satan's attack on my throat was likely in response to my most recent bout of verbal attack on him, and I would have to fight through the pain of that and keep reciting them. I was going to pound Satan with the hammer of the Word until he turned my body loose.

As soon as I began to gather my weapons, the enemy increased the pain.

The fight was on.

THE FIGHT AGAINST HOPELESSNESS

One of the biggest battles I faced as I pressed in for the healing revelation that would set me free was the battle against hopelessness. As you face day after day of constant pain, it wears away at your will. It takes your joy and your rest and wears you down physically as well as mentally.

In the Bible, there is a scripture that talks about the enemy wearing down the saints in the end times. I studied that verse some in May of 2019 just before I updated this book and discovered the phrase "wearing down" actually meant: wearing down, wearing out and to harass continually." A day or so after I discovered those meanings, a gentleman emailed and told me of some old sin thoughts he was battling. One night the Lord told him he was being tormented by a Demon of Harassment. Demons are often tormenting spirits. I believe demons that bring pain are tormentors. It is up to us to stop them by commanding them to leave us in Jesus Name.

When every moment is filled with suffering, and when nothing you do seems to make any difference, you get weaker as each new day dawns. I fought this battle extra hard during this time period.

Praise is always part of our arsenal when we are battling against the enemy. Praising God shows Him our trust is in Him, and that we know our help is going to come from Him.

I fought by praising and thanking God for my complete healing, for the fact that many thousands of my brothers and sisters in Christ would be healed with the revelations He would give me for this book, because that was *His* promise to me. (You can always war against the enemy with God's promises to you, and true prophetic words God has given you, as well).

I praised Him for the fact that Jesus already purchased my healing and that I had the easy part - all I had to do was drive out the lies of the enemy and the truth of my healing would spring forth. It made me think of this verse from Isaiah:

Isaiah 58:8

Then shall thy light break forth as the morning, and thine health shall spring forth speedily: and thy righteousness shall go before thee; the glory of the LORD shall be thy rearward.

Once I drove out the lies of the enemy, my health *would* spring forth, I knew it would. The Lord had told me the pain I was in was only for the purpose of writing this book, and I believed Him.

Others urged me to find new doctors and get pain medication, but I knew the Lord would not allow anyone to solve my problem when He was trying to get a revelation to me. He wanted to heal me Himself, and doctors so far had only cost me money, they had offered almost no relief at all from the pain. I felt my time would be better spent studying healing than chasing after more doctors. I already had God's Word on my situation. I knew He would be faithful to keep it. He always was. No one else's word mattered to me.

That weekend, I began to press in with even more determination for the truth about how to destroy the enemy's lies about my healing. I knew somewhere there was a key to receiving the full manifestation of healing in my body. The enemy continued to try increasing the symptoms of strep throat on me and I fought back hard. For days, it had been a stalemate between us. I had not been able to make the symptoms completely disappear, but he had not been able to make the illness completely manifest, either, so I felt at least that was a good sign. Every time the pain increased, I went after him, warring against his attack with the Word of God and with tongues.

I wasn't making as much progress on the pain in my spine. I continued to declare that I was healed by the stripes of Jesus, and to try to see myself healed in my mind. The pain became overwhelming at various times of the day, leaving me unable to even sit still. I would walk the floor and pray, try to distract myself with some other activity, or if it became unbearable, lie down for a little while to get a break from it.

But I wanted total victory. I didn't want the enemy to be able to put *any* pain or sickness on me, and I knew there was a way to have that. I knew if the enemy could find a way to put me to bed for good, he would. He knew that any revelation I got, I would share with as many of my brothers and sisters in Christ as possible.

Over the weekend and through Monday, I continued studying healing teachings by others and fighting the pain by confessing the Word of God out loud and speaking to my spine and shoulders that they were healed in the Name of Jesus and by His stripes and the blood He shed on the cross. The pain had been awful all weekend, which I attributed to the fact that I was fighting harder to replace the enemy's lies with the truth of God's Word.

I had noticed over the weekend a difference in when I just confessed I was healed by the stripes of Jesus, and when I spoke directly to the body part in pain and commanded it to line up with the Word of God.

When I spoke directly to the body part and commanded it,

the pain receded slightly. This happened every time, so I had begun doing that more frequently.

I would curse the affliction and speak death to it, then tell the body part it was healed, command it to line up with the Word of God and be healed in the Name of Jesus, and I would speak that I applied the shed Blood of Jesus to it, and then I would follow by speaking life to it.

Every time I repeated this process, I would feel the pain recede for a few seconds, so I knew I was on to something. I also prayed in the spirit a lot during these times of confession and speaking to my body. I decided to continue this method of fighting until the Lord showed me something different to do.

Monday night of the holiday weekend, the Lord spoke to me again.

Press in for your healing, daughter, for you shall surely receive it in every part of your body, and a bonus besides.

Speak My Name, declare My glory reigns in you, and healing courses through your veins, for I have already healed you and it is manifesting already!

Don't stop speaking My Word just because you do not yet see any results, for truly I tell you, it is working in you even now to heal you.

Just as the fig tree died from the roots up, so shall this affliction also. Many of My children give up after confessing My Word only once or twice, and this should not be. They believe only what they see, and without faith they cannot see the manifestation of My promises in their lives.

Let this not be so in your life, child, for I desire greatly that you would receive the gift of healing My Son purchased for you with His own Blood. I desire all My children would receive it and walk in health at all times, that their joy may be full, that others may see how I bless those who follow Me.

Press in, My daughter. I will give you short breaks from the intense suffering that you may write and do other tasks, only do not stop pressing in, for the enemy seeks to torment you for all you have done in My Name, and he will if you do not receive your healing.

Mark 11:20

And in the morning, as they passed by, they saw the fig tree dried up from the roots.

After that night, I began declaring as the Lord had instructed me, in addition to speaking to the afflicted parts of my body and praying in the spirit.

One afternoon that next week, I was walking through my house after answering an email to a friend who asked about my pain level. I had answered honestly. I had been studying how others had received the full manifestation of their healing. All of them kept their confession in line with God's Word. They declared themselves healed and blessed. They never said they were sick or in pain.

Suddenly, I remembered something the Lord spoke to me the previous year when I was praying for a complaining friend. She constantly complained about everything in her life from her marriage that ended forty years earlier. to her present family relationships, to her pain and illness. It made enjoying her company impossible.

One night, I was praying for the Lord to help her, when the Lord spoke to me.

Every time she speaks her pain or misery, she establishes it.

It was clear He greatly desired to heal her, that He did not want her to be miserable and in pain. I saw in my spirit that her words kept Him from being able to bless her. I was reminded of a verse in Malachi.

Malachi 3:13

Your words have been stout against me, saith the LORD. Yet ye say, What have we spoken so much against thee?

The Lord had told me to study how others had received their healing and to do the same steps, and He had said He would teach me more as I did those things.

I knew I had not kept my confession positive. My pain level had been so intense in multiple areas that I had not held back saying so, although saying so had not helped it improve any. In fact, it had helped it to get worse. **If every time my friend spoke about her pain she established it, that meant every time I spoke mine, I was also establishing it.** The last thing I wanted to do was give my already soaring pain level more strength. I didn't want to build it up, I wanted to tear it down!

I decided the next day I would not speak a single negative word out of my mouth about the pain I was dealing with, and I wouldn't write one in any emails, either, no matter how severe it got. I knew writing and speaking weren't the same, but writing it made me think about it, so at the very least, it affected what was on my mind screen, and that was another area I had been working on. My pain level was already so bad that on many days I was fighting back tears as I tried to get my work done, so I knew the next day could become very challenging, but I was determined.

All throughout the next day and evening, I was careful not to speak anything about what I felt physically, and not to write anything about it either. That evening, I was sitting at my computer answering emails when I realized my pain level had continually lessened as the day wore on. I had used my usual over the counter remedies - double doses of Naproxen and capsaicin patches, but I had far less pain than any of the preceding days when I had been using the same remedies. In fact, I had changed the pain patch less often on that day than on any preceding days since my battle with pain had begun.

Every hour that passed without me speaking and helping establish the pain the enemy wanted me in seemed to be helping to defeat him!

That night, when I removed the pain patch prior to taking a shower, I noticed spots of blood on it. Why would I be bleeding when I had done nothing to break my skin? I knew that couldn't be a good sign. Only one thing was likely to cause that - a skin infection. As I held up my mirror, I saw a rash had appeared under the pain patch. I knew I had been extra careful to remove all the capsaicin residue every night before applying a fresh patch. There was no logical reason for me to have a rash.

I tried not to panic as I realized I would not be able to put another patch on. The patches had been my best source of pain relief during my months of pain. Now I would have to rely solely on the Naproxen, a change I did not relish at all. I began praying.

Lord, I know what that rash is......

Is that an acceptable illness, daughter?

No, Lord. No illness is acceptable to me now that I know I am healed!

I realized then what the enemy was doing. He was trying to tempt me to accept an illness I had experienced before, to see if I would take it! He knew I was busy fighting pain and he had slipped one in behind my back. Literally.

Immediately I came against the infection and commanded it to leave, declaring to my back it was healed and I would not accept any illness, any infection *or* any pain.

Okay, Lord, Your Word says He bore my griefs and carried my sorrows. I know those words mean sickness and pain as well as grief and sorrow, so that means Jesus already carried away my pain. He carried it off at the cross, and that means I don't have to also carry it, so I'm claiming Isaiah 53:4 as my pain patch now. If He carried it, I don't have to!

I was seeing the Word of God working in my situation, and I was getting bolder. As soon as I spoke that prayer, the pain receded, but I knew the enemy well enough to know he never went down without a fight.

The next day I continued to confess Isaiah 53:4 and declare my healing. That night, when I undressed to shower, I felt a sensation on my back. Holding up the mirror, I saw not only was the rash still there, but it had worsened - considerably. It had now spread across my back and was several times worse. As if to announce its presence more boldly, it began to cause a burning sensation. I had refused to speak its name out loud, or tell anyone, even though I knew exactly what it appeared to be. I only knew of one type of infection ever caused that burning feeling.

...if you give it a name, then you gave it a place. (John W. Morgan)

Oh no you don't, Satan! I will not accept any infection, any illness, or any pain - not now and not ever again!

I realized in my busyness that day that I had forgotten to speak to my back that it was healed. I had declared my pain was gone, but I hadn't spoken to my body. I was slacking on my consistency and that had left a crack for the enemy to attack me through.

I immediately began speaking to it and telling it to line up with the Word of God and telling it that it was healed. I also cursed the infection and rash and commanded it to leave my body in the Name of Jesus.

As I prepared myself for bed hours later, I again spoke to my back and commanded it to line up with the Word of God. I confessed that healing was flowing through my veins and the Lord of Glory reigned in me. As I prayed, a sharp pain arose in one knee.

Does he never stop?

But I knew the answer to that question, even as I thought it in my frustration.

I reached for the anointing oil on my dresser and began to pray as I anointed the knee.

Lord, Your Word says in James Chapter 5 to anoint with oil those that are sick and that the prayer of faith will raise them up. I'm anointing this knee right now!

I began confessing Isaiah 53:4 over the knee and commanding

the pain to leave it in Jesus Name. Over and over I spoke the same command, the same scripture. After several minutes, the pain left. I decided to anoint my back, too, just for good measure, and I repeated the process with my back.

Realize when you start fighting for your healing that you *will* have to fight. The enemy will not give up making you sick or in pain without trying everything he can to get you to keep at least one or two of your illnesses or pains first. He'll try anything you've had before, gotten this time of year, that runs in your family or that you've read about lately in a magazine or heard about on television that he thinks you might go for. **Believing God's Word can manifest healing in your body will be a fight if you've believed the enemy's word to manifest sickness all the years up til now.**

One thing I noticed as I fought the enemy day after day to establish my healing was that the more I confessed Isaiah 53:4 out loud, the more righteous anger rose up in my spirit every time the enemy tried to strike me again. **The more you realize healing is yours and that it has been ever since you gave your life to Jesus, the more righteous anger will rise up in you at the enemy.** This anger is useful to you in battle – use it!

When I first began my battle to establish God's healing power in my body, I was in pain and fighting the enemy was the last thing I felt like doing. For weeks, my fight was feeble, but as I began to see even the tiniest traces of victory, I was strengthened and encouraged.

Nothing compares to the thrill of victory when you begin winning this battle! When God's healing power begins manifesting as you drive out the lies of the enemy, the thrill of victory will surge through you and make you fight even harder.

Don't be afraid you don't have enough strength to do the battle – healing is a journey, and it is on the journey that He gives you strength. It is God's will you win the battle for your health and He will strengthen you as you take even small steps towards the goal! His strength is made perfect in your weakness!

Joel 3:10

Beat your plowshares into swords and your pruninghooks into spears: let the weak say, I am strong.

The context of this scripture is warfare, and you can use it to war against the illness in your body. Say you are strong and keep fighting! The prize is walking every day in radiant health, without pain!

The enemy may hit you with one thing after another after another, like he did me, but it doesn't matter - God's Word is like one-stop shopping. It encompasses everything!

I was so encouraged by the continued manifestation of my healing that the following day, I decided if Isaiah 53:4 was strong enough to replace my pain patches, it was certainly strong enough to replace the Naproxen as well. I stopped taking them.

Over the next couple of days, the pain would increase at various times and I was tempted to take the Naproxen. Whenever it increased, I stopped whatever I was doing and warred against it with the sword of the Word.

MY WARFARE PRAYER

Lord, Your Word is absolute truth. If Isaiah 53:4 is my pain patch, then it covers all my pain, not just part of it. I refuse to take Naproxen to get pain relief that Jesus took a horrible lashing to get for me!

Pain, in the Name of Jesus, I command you to leave my body now! I apply Isaiah 53:4 to you. I apply the Blood of Jesus to you. I am a healed child of God and you are trespassing! You are a lie from the pit of hell and I won't stand for you tormenting me any longer! He carried my griefs, my sorrows, my pain and my sickness *when He went to the cross! I don't have to carry them ever again! Go **now**!*

I repeated the commands over several times. The pain was not completely gone, but I sat back down and resumed my writing. It left within minutes.

Though there were short bouts of pain here and there over the next few days, overall the pain and symptoms continued to decrease as I continued to destroy the lies of the enemy and establish the truth of my healing with God's Word. Each time the pain increased, I warred against it.

The infection, too, decreased day by day. Normally that type of skin infection increases, causes great pain and necessitates a visit to the doctor and strong antibiotics. This time, God's Word proved to be much stronger than any antibiotic, and each day I continued to see improvement. I refused to see a doctor for the rash when I knew I was already healed.

During this time, the truth of God's healing power really took root in my spirit. Where before it had been something I only knew in my mind, now it became alive and active in my entire being.

Whenever a symptom would arise in my body before, I would immediately think of what medicine or supplement I could take to try to remedy it. Now, with the word of healing firmly rooting in my spirit, His Word would rise up in me and answer the symptom or illness or pain, driving it from my body. **The Word of God is alive inside you, and His power is unstoppable!**

Over this time period, I had lost more mobility in my left arm. It would raise to just under shoulder level and no higher, and even that far brought pain. The right shoulder was trying to follow suit. Laying in bed late one night, I decided to press in to manifest healing in my shoulders next. I began to speak out loud to my shoulders and command them to be healed in the Name of Jesus and line up with the Word of God.

101

Someone online had suggested I might have "frozen shoulder," which is apparently when scar tissue takes your mobility and causes terrible pain in your shoulder. I didn't know what I had, only that the pain was unbearable. Just in case, I commanded any scar tissue in them to die and dissolve and come out of my body, and I cursed whatever affliction was causing the immobility and commanded it to die and leave as well.

Waking up really early the next morning, something didn't feel normal. I had that feeling that you get when you wake up in a strange place, just before your brain remembers that you're on vacation.

Then I realized I was laying on my right shoulder.

For months, I had struggled to sleep comfortably laying flat on my back. It was indeed a struggle, because I am a side sleeper. Whenever I would try to sleep on either side, though, the pain in my shoulders would be unbearable, no matter how many pillows I used, and I had given up even trying, resigning myself to the insomnia brought on by discomfort.

It had been months since I had slept on my side. In previous months, any time I turned on my side while sleeping, the intense pain it brought would immediately wake me up.

I had been sleeping on my side! The Word had worked again! I was overjoyed the power of God's Word was working so quickly. I knew His truth had taken hold in my spirit and that what I was learning would help thousands of others.

I had wondered as I began my healing journey, how many times I would have to confess His Word before I saw results. I knew I had ailments I had been claiming for decades. Once I had even prayed about it.

Lord, am I going to have to make a positive confession of Your Word once for every time I made a negative one claiming an illness or condition in the past?

Silence.

He had not answered my question. Now I saw the answer.

Receiving the manifestation of my healing wasn't about how many times, or even how often I confessed His word. It was about how deeply I *understood* and *believed* that I was already healed.

CHAPTER 21 – OUTSIDE INFLUENCES

One day in May, I was talking to Mom on the phone when she casually remarked how I had always been sickly. God suddenly showed me truth where before I had been seeing only a lie.

Not wanting to disrespect her, I said nothing, but I silently prayed against those words in my mind, not letting them take root. As quickly as I could, I got off the phone call and launched an all-out attack, canceling the power of the negative words, commanding any curse they had brought to be broken off, and commanding all demonic influence let in by either to return to hell where it belonged.

The words we speak to and over our children and loved ones are so important. My Mom would never have spoken that had she understood the power of those words. I had allowed them all those years because I had not realized their power, either.

I realized my Mom had been telling me I was sick my entire life. I remembered being a small child and hearing that I was a nervous child and always sickly. Looking back over my childhood, I was healthy and very active the majority of the time, but her words had an effect. Somewhere along the way, they had taken root and I had begun to see myself as sickly. Consequently, around the same time, I began to suffer from one illness and infection after another. In fact, by the time I was 12 years old, every cut on a fence I got, every time I stepped on a thorn, any type of injury I got, it would set up blood poisoning and as soon as we saw the tell-tell red line, Mom would rush me to the doctor.

I had wondered for years why my immune system seemed so weak, when I took vitamins and supplements daily trying to strengthen it.

I knew I had to tear down that image of myself and put a healthy one in its place. I had put pictures of me when I was healthy and well around where I spent most of my time, to help establish a well and healthy image of myself in my mind. This seemed to help a lot. I also began to spend a few minutes each day in the morning and in the evening remembering times when I was healthy and active and really concentrating on that image.

What I call the mind screen is simply your imagination. Seeing yourself as well and healthy and not ill is an extremely important part of receiving the full manifestation of your healing. **What your mind screen is showing you is what your body will manifest, good or bad. It is what you truly believe, what you have put your faith in, and what you are expecting, regardless of what your words say about where your faith is**. It is imperative that you get your self image to line up with God's Word that you are healed.

One important factor in this, i**t is very difficult to see yourself healed when everyone around you sees you as sick**.

If you are dealing with a long standing illness or long-term condition, this will likely require much effort on your part. How to handle the family and friends who see you as ill is something you may want to pray about, but most of all, keep *your* confession in line with God's Word, and keep the picture on your mind screen a healthy one. This is very important to the success of manifesting your healing. You may need to explain to them why you are talking health and not sickness so they can help you reach your healing goal.

Our loved ones mean well when they give us their input on the condition of our health, but unless their input lines up with the Word of God, it is not conducive to you receiving your healing.

Time went on, and I was working every possible moment of the day. By late June, I was producing two weekly radio shows, plus working on the books the Lord wanted me to write, and ministering to many listeners online and by video when one morning, I woke up in pain. The pain wasn't severe, just bothersome. It was a pain I had felt before. The chiropractor had told me it usually meant I had at least one rib out of place due to a misalignment in my spine.

I began trying to confess that I was healed and I realized I could no longer remember the scriptures and now I felt no authority rise up in me when I tried to rebuke the pain. I had stopped confessing them when my physical pain had diminished enough I could function normally because I had multiple projects pressing in on me, and so much work that needed to be done each day. I had stopped fighting for my healing because I had begun to feel well.

I realized then that I had allowed Mark 4:19 to happen to me - the cares of the world had risen up and choked out the healing Word of God in me and now I could no longer remember it. Now I was trying to do battle with a rusty sword.

Mark 4:18-19

18 And these are they which are sown among thorns; such as hear the word,

19 And the cares of this world, and the deceitfulness of riches, and the lusts of other things entering in, choke the word, and it becometh unfruitful.

Now I would have to begin all over again, and it was my own fault. The next morning, I went through my Bible with Post-It tabbies and I tabbed every healing scripture, speaking them out loud as I went, praying them over myself.

It is very important once you get the revelation and are seeing results, that you do *not* let the enemy steal the Word from you or you won't have it when you need it most.

As life went on, I went back and forth between believing I was healed and forgetting I was healed in my usual busyness.

The Lord had told me I would be completely healed in the future. I knew from God that healing was supposed to be part of the ministry I did while at Princeton, and He had told me that my healing would be the first one. I looked forward to being healed of everything. It had been so many years since I had been pain-free that I had long ago lost count.

As usual, I was so busy I felt as if I was working two jobs all the time. In the natural, I had given up my secular job the year before at the Lord's direction to finish the first book on time, and devote my life to ministry, but the constant influx of emails plus producing two radio shows a week and working on multiple books kept me up working until the wee hours of the morning every night, almost every night of the week.

Eventually, the pain I was dealing with lessened somewhat, and my attention drifted to a series I began on Blog Talk Radio and the books I was writing.

With everything I had going on, I was busy from the time I woke up each morning until I fell into an exhausted sleep each night.

One morning in late November, I woke up and talked on the phone for awhile and then fell back asleep. I awoke again later needing to get up.

When I stood up to get out of bed, I fell. I tried and tried to pull myself back up by the bed post, but my arms would not pull me up. I scolded myself for not pushing harder in my daily workout and kept trying.

I thought of lying down and rolling over and getting up on all fours, but when I tried, I couldn't remember how to do it, so I tried again to grab something on my bed frame to get up. The phone rang again and again and I desperately tried to reach my phone on the nightstand but it was too far away. Then the other phone started to ring a VOIP line I used as a backup when my cell phone was down and I could not reach that one either.

When the second line started ringing, my son who shared a house with me knocked on my door and I called out to him. He knew I always answered my phone. He pushed the door open a crack.

"Mom, are you okay?"

"I fell and I can't get up - can you help me up? I really need to go to the bathroom!"

"Mom, have you taken any medicines? Any drugs?" (My son knew I didn't do recreational drugs, but he knew something was very, very wrong with me because of my very slurred speech, and he didn't know what else to think.)

"No, of course not! I'm fine, I just fell and can't get up. This is what I get for not working out!"

"I know, I know, but I had to ask. Mom, you've had a stroke, I'm calling 911."

He quickly realized from my slurred speech what had happened. Although I heard the slur in my words, my brain wasn't registering that it meant something was very wrong with me. I felt fine, I just couldn't get up out of the floor.

"I don't need an ambulance, I just need to get up out of the floor so I can go to the bathroom."

My son then came into my room and picked me up under the arms and carried me to the toilet. He is six feet tall and very strong and that day I was more than a little glad of it.

"Don't get up by yourself! You call me when you're done and I'll come get you!" he said and he walked out, closing the door behind him.

I was certain I was just fine. I was not calling my grown son to help me off the toilet! I went to stand up and promptly fell again. Thank God I didn't strike my head on anything in either fall.

It seemed like only seconds later when EMT's appeared in my bathroom and started asking me questions and cutting my long nightgown off me.

"We're taking you to the hospital in McKinney and they are going to put you in a room in ICU," one of them said.

I felt fine, I didn't understand why everyone was making such a fuss over me, but I wasn't going to argue with trained professionals. If they thought I should go to the hospital and be checked out, then I would go there. I was sure it wouldn't take long.

"Y'all need to give that room in ICU to someone who is sick. I'm not sick, I just fell," I told them.

They exchanged glances, smiling.

Then they put a board under me and slid me onto the gurney and into the back of an ambulance. All I remember of the ride was hearing a very loud siren for a few seconds, then I lost consciousness.

At the hospital, when the doctor spoke to my son after the initial exam, he told him honestly they didn't know if they could save me or not. A blood vessel in my brain had burst and was bleeding into my brain and its location made it inoperable.

The bleed was too deep for them to operate. What was more, the doctor said that if the bleed reached my brain stem, it would stop my heart and respiratory system.

I don't remember the Emergency Room and the hourly CT Scans they did on me other than a very bright light and a very unfriendly looking doctor asking me roughly if I knew where I was and I answered, "Yes, I'm at home," to which he replied, "No, you're in the Emergency Room," and I said, "I am?" I remember his face and eyes did not seem kind, but I did not have the strength to care as I slipped back into unconsciousness.

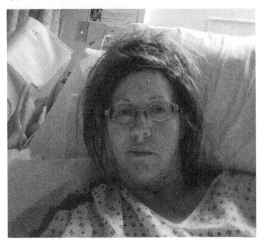

In the hospital – Late 2012

The CT Scans showed I had suffered a hemorrhagic stroke in the right side of my brain that affected the left side of my body.

From November 27th until December 7th, I was in that hospital, before being moved to a rehab hospital for a week of physical and speech therapy. Initially, my left side was almost completely paralyzed, which was why I hadn't been able to get myself up out of the floor when I fell.

One day in that first week, I was alone in my hospital room, and I began to pray.

Lord, I don't know why this stroke happened, I must have opened a door to the enemy somewhere, but I trust You with the outcome.

I praise You for the stroke, Lord. It could not have happened without You allowing it, so I am believing You to bring good out of it.

I did not give God praise for the stroke with great joy, but I was determined to praise Him, regardless. He always knows what we don't about a situation, and no matter where we are, He is still God, and He still deserves our praise. I hoped He would bring some good out of it.

After the three weeks, I was sent home to recover on my own. I had to use a walker to get around, something I never in my wildest thoughts imagined myself doing. At the hospital I moved around in a wheelchair or on the walker only. I wasn't allowed to bathe or shower without someone in the room with me in case I fell, I couldn't bend forward, cry or get congested from anything because of the effect on intracranial pressure, so it was a problem to pick up the things I was constantly dropping with my left hand. To add to my misery, the hip-length light auburn hair that I had spent ten years growing out was in a giant matted ball on the back of my head where it had been since I first regained consciousness in my room at the hospital however many days it was after the stroke when I awoke. The doctors must have been afraid to let anyone braid it or clip it up and now it looked and felt like a big ball of matted dog hair. I had tried to comb some of it out and so had others, but to no avail. I wondered if my hair would have to be shaved off my head now since it could not be combed.

Glynda Lomax

My hair just months before the stroke

I still had very little actual understanding of what had happened to me, or how serious it really was.

My first week home, I went to my hairdresser and she and two other hairdressers tugged and pulled on my long hair for four hours to comb most of it out until the pain was so intense I could stand no more. I lost about half of it in the process, there just wasn't any other way to get the tangles out except to tear the hair out with them. What was left was in a million different lengths. Still, any other hairdresser would have insisted on just cutting it off at the hairline. I thanked God I had one that cared. She knew from cutting my hair for the past year how I tried to take care of it and leave all the length on it I could each time, and she went the extra mile. I loved my long hair and I desperately wanted to keep it. I had always wanted hair that long, and this was the only time I had been able to grow it all the way out, at the age of 52.

For weeks after coming home, I was so weak that getting up and walking across a room left me exhausted for hours. Trying to dress myself was a major undertaking. I found I could only put on the loosest fitting, easiest-to-put-on garments because of having such limited mobility. Since I looked almost as bad as I felt, it didn't matter much. I really couldn't go many places anyway. Driving was out of the question.

I had no appetite at all and most days in the beginning weeks, forcing down five small bites was the total of my food intake for the day, but the doctors had continually told me that eating, resting and doing the prescribed exercises were the biggest factors in how fast and how much I would recover, so I kept trying to force even small amounts of food down as often as I could. Since the left side of my throat was numb along with much of the left side of my body, forcing food down often resulted in choking. I had eaten well at the hospital, but at home I could not prepare food like I usually did, so I relied on frozen dinners and things that were easy to prepare and not very tasty.

Even the simplest tasks had become so difficult, I wanted to curl up in bed and never get up again. I couldn't take a shower without someone in the room. I couldn't hold a thought for even a minute. I wasn't able to get up and write and I was too weak to do a podcast. I fought back – hard. I worked my physical therapy harder, I prayed harder, I tried to see myself healed and active again.

The whole time, I was terrified I would never really see myself that way again in reality. The battle between my thoughts and what I saw in my body was constant....and exhausting.

Friends of the ministry knew what had happened to me, since I had sent them a mailing when my son brought my laptop to the hospital, but now I wasn't able to even produce content for them. How long would I be so helpless and unable to do the ministry? I didn't want to let God down. I didn't want to disappoint my listeners. What if they all went away? I felt so helpless. I couldn't even drive to the grocery store or post office!

My first night home, after heating a dinner in the microwave, I had dropped my left hand in it while fixing a cup of coffee with my right and didn't know until I felt it burning a few minutes later. Having so much numbness in my left side was a real problem in the kitchen. It was a problem no matter what I was trying to do.

I had hired my brother and sister-in-law to help me several days a week in the beginning, to go to the grocery store, prepare food, do housework for me and do errands, since I could do almost nothing. At first I could only be up a little while during the day, my strength was so small.

Every day, I would lay on my bed for hours, staring at the walls and thinking of all I needed to be up doing that I could not do. The deficit in my left side had reduced my almost 100wpm typing speed to one finger hunt and peck typing. I already had over two hundred unanswered emails, with more coming in every day.

Any time I got up to walk, I had to take hyper-vigilant care not to stumble over my dragging left foot or lose my balance and fall. A fall could restart the bleeding, since the blown blood vessel could not be repaired. The last thing I wanted was to go back to the hospital. I just wanted to get well and get my life back.

Please, Lord, help me to receive healing and get back to work ministering to Your people!

Everything in my life seemed so dark and so difficult. I wanted desperately to kneel down and pour out my heart and my tears to God, but I could neither kneel nor cry yet so I just held it inside.

Day after day, I fought to get stronger. I did my physical therapy exercises even though I hated how they exhausted me after even the first few minutes. I never knew a stroke could affect so much.

One evening, after fighting a bottle of pills open, I was shuffling slowly towards the kitchen carrying them so I could take one when I lost my grip and dropped the bottle. Pills scattered everywhere as I looked on helplessly, wondering how I would stoop to pick them all up without bending forward. Why did everything have to be so challenging?

I fought back tears as I got as near the floor as I could without bending forward and began picking up my medicine. When I finished, I called my local drugstore and requested only flip-top caps so I would never had to leave another cap off again.

As I lay on my bed day after day willing myself to heal, I often wondered if I would ever regain all I had lost. Nothing in my life felt normal any more. I had to hire people to clean, grocery shop and drive me around. To add to that, I was treated like a child, as if the stroke had turned me into an idiot.

I couldn't clean my house. I couldn't work on the books because I could barely type and sitting up for even an hour wore me completely out. What little I could type was almost all typos that had to be corrected, so even answering one email was exhausting.

Texting on my phone was pretty much the same. My body just would not obey my brain. How would I do podcasts with such a weak voice? What if I never regained all my abilities? How would I survive? How would I write?

I began working harder than ever each day to strengthen my left hand. I forced myself to try to type with both hands, even though the last two fingers of my left kept dragging and holding down keys, making whole lines of a single letter, or adding big space gaps where they didn't belong. Still, I didn't see any way to improve without practicing, even though practicing also exhausted me. Typing, texting and talking on the phone all wore me out quickly, presumably because of the mental energy they required.

In just a matter of minutes, my life had gone from normal to constant rehabilitation and trying to heal, unable to do my daily work, I felt as if I had not laughed in months.

On the third morning home from the hospital, I woke up at 5:30 a.m. As I lay still trying to go back to sleep, I began praying.

Lord God in heaven, there is nothing You can't do. Please help me get better. Everything is so hard now, and there is so little I can do for myself. Please help me!

To my delight, He answered me very clearly.

I will restore you to 100% function, with a bonus, because you praised Me for the stroke - but you must see yourself well.

Wow! A bonus, too? I had remembered to praise Him, although I knew I had not done it with great joy. I did do it believing He would bring good out of the stroke somehow.

Part of the frustration of those first months was that I wasn't supposed to cry, and I wanted so desperately to cry. I wanted to cry out to God in my helplessness, my fear, and my frustration. But I knew if I cried, it would increase intracranial pressure and I could stroke again, so I didn't.

Normally, if I was in pain, I went aside with the Lord and cried out to Him in prayer. I was in terrible emotional pain during the months following the stroke. I felt so alone and afraid. I had never been unable to work and take care of myself. What if I never fully recovered? I was so afraid I would lose all my listeners. Who would I minister to if they all went away because I could not answer their emails yet or produce podcasts?

I would make my way slowly to the kitchen in an attempt to make myself some instant hot cereal and the first thing I would do was drop the bowl on the floor. All day long when I would finally muster the strength to get up and try to walk on my walker, I would manage to make my way into this room or that one, I would drop things, and since I wasn't supposed to bend forward, I could not pick them up. I had tried lowering myself straight down and back up to retrieve them, but the action made me almost pass out with lightheadedness. I was beyond frustrated.

The future at that point looked so dark. I desperately wished I could just go to bed and never get up again, but I loved Jesus and my children and grandchildren too much to give up the fight to get well, or to give up. And I desperately wanted to finish the work the Lord had assigned to me. I wanted my life to count for something when it was all said and done. Something for the Kingdom of God. I just had to keep trying.

I could neither get on my knees nor pour out my heart and tears, so I fought back the tears and kept on praying. At least I knew for sure now that I would regain all my function.

My sister who had herself suffered a number of Ischemic strokes had reminded me more than once that one of my neurologists at the hospital had told me it would probably take me 8 months to regain 80% of my function. I believed that was the prognosis for a person with my condition who was *not* a believer, not for me, and I said so as he spoke it as well as every time she reminded me of it, telling them both respectfully that I served a God who could and would do much better than that! I would most certainly *not* take 8 months to get that much better! The devil *was* a liar!

Something else related to healing that I learned in this time was about jesting. Jesting, meaning joking, is also speaking. It took me decades to realize what the Bible meant by coarse jesting, and why it is a problem. Especially since it is so obvious the Lord has a sense of humor.

Ephesians 5:1-7

Glynda Lomax

1 Be ye therefore followers of God, as dear children;

2 And walk in love, as Christ also hath loved us, and hath given himself for us an offering and a sacrifice to God for a sweet smelling savour.

3 But fornication, and all uncleanness, or covetousness, let it not be once named Among you, as becometh saints;

4 Neither filthiness, nor foolish talking, nor jesting, which are not convenient: but rather giving of thanks.

5 For this ye know, that no whoremonger, nor unclean person, nor covetous man, who is an idolater, hath any inheritance in the kingdom of Christ and of God.

6 Let no man deceive you with vain words: for because of these things cometh the wrath of God upon the children of disobedience.

7 Be not ye therefore partakers with them.

I had wondered many times while reading that scripture why it was not okay to make jokes. One day as I was studying healing, the Lord brought some of the things I used to jest about to my remembrance. Clarity hit my mind then – hard.

Years ago, I had an expression. "He was so mad, he looked like he was gonna pop a vein!"

Do you know what causes a hemorrhagic stroke? A vein bursts.

The Lord showed me that any time we make jokes about our own or anyone else's health, even though we are only joking, it opens a door to the enemy in that area of *our* bodies.

CALLING THINGS

One night I lay in bed listening to a CD about calling those things that be not, and I began thinking about my situation.

What have I been calling these things, Lord?

To my dismay, I realized I was so miserable in my body, and so frustrated in my emotions, that I had been calling things the way they were. I knew better than that! The Lord had taught me a few years before that whenever we speak our misery, we establish it in our reality because we are decreeing it.

Job 22:28

Thou shalt also decree a thing, and it shall be established unto thee: and the light shall shine upon thy ways.

I didn't want to establish my misery, I wanted to come out of it, to recover.

Okay, Lord, starting tomorrow morning, I'm changing my confession! I'm going to confess I'm getting better and stronger every day!

Starting the next morning, every time someone called or emailed and asked me how I was doing, I replied I was getting stronger every day, that I was constantly improving.

Every day, I tried to stay up longer, to do more activities, though the fatigue was awful. It was up to me if I wanted to get well. I desperately wanted to be working on the books the Lord had me writing.

Since I couldn't seem to type anything but typos because of my left hand malfunctioning, I tried to content myself with hand writing notes on a tablet instead. At least I could still write manually with no problem. It was the closest I could come to working with my left side deficit. My brain seemed well enough to want to work, just not well enough to perform the work. I remembered the nurses at the hospital were shocked I could still speak and write when I came out of the coma, and I was just grateful I still *could* work.

Days later, I realized suddenly I felt strength coming into my body. It was a huge improvement.

At first I didn't understand why I felt strength for the first time since the stroke because I was barely eating a fifth of a skinny girl's food and even that I was having to force down. I had been losing weight at a rapid pace which, before the stroke, would have delighted me to no end.

Then I remembered I had changed my confession, and I knew the only thing I had changed was my confession. **It was so exciting to see the power of my own confession literally bringing strength to my body!**

Every day I continued confessing …. and I continued improving.

Thank You, Lord, for giving Your children this ability to speak and change our situations!

Proverbs 12:18

There is that speaketh like the piercings of a sword: but the tongue of the wise is health.

I had latched onto another scripture, too, listening to Bible teachings when I was resting:

Proverbs 12:6

The words of the wicked are to lie in wait for blood: but the mouth of the upright shall deliver them.

I had never seen the power of words manifested so quickly and so powerfully as I was seeing it now, literally bringing health to my body! The thought that my mouth could deliver me was an exciting one.

One of the greatest hindrances I encountered when pressing in for healing was fighting the fear that attacked me again and again in times of compromised health or great pain. I feared the intense pain would never cease, and after the stroke I desperately feared being permanently disabled. I was so afraid I might never walk again without a walker, or never drive again. How could I possibly take care of myself if I could not walk or drive?

After the stroke, members of my family thought I should apply for Social Security Disability. I didn't, but I prayed about it to be sure. The Lord confirmed I should not – for two reasons; 1. He was going to completely heal me, and 2. He told me I would *internalize* that label if I did apply. He showed me I would 'see' myself as disabled forever if I applied, thus setting up a stronghold in my mind which would exalt itself against the truth of God's Word that I was healed. I chose not to apply for any disability. I would trust God. He had never let me down before, I knew He would not begin now. (This is not imply that others should not apply, only that it was the right choice for me not to. Since I teach about God's Word, this was the right choice for me.)

Any person who is diagnosed with a serious illness or who lives with intense pain will experience some level of fear. When my Dad was dying of lung cancer, he had told me once he wasn't afraid of death, but he *was* afraid of what might lay between where he was and death's door - the pain. As it turned out in his case, there was a lot to fear. He suffered horribly before cancer finally ended his life in April of 1999.

There had been times over past years when some situation would come up that needed to be solved and as I would begin to pray over it, faith would rise up inside me like a tidal wave. That sometimes happens when sickness or pain attacks me as well.

When we truly get inside us that healing is ours, that will begin happening *every* time we are faced with a physical attack. God's Word is alive and when we take it in, it literally *abides* or lives in us. Once you get to this point, His Word will rise up in you and answer the sickness or pain for you! When you feel that faith rise up in you, remember this verse:

Hebrews 11:1

Now faith is the substance of things hoped for, the evidence of things not seen.

I believe when I feel faith rise up in me that it is God's signal to me that I already have what I need. That faith is my evidence (substance) that victory (the thing hoped for in this verse, the end result I can't see yet – in this case, healing) is already ordained by Him. It is the sign that everything is going to be okay.

So faith rising up in you like that is your signal God wants to do something for you in your situation.

The reverse is also true. **Any time fear rises up in us, it should make us realize there is something that God wants us to have that the enemy is trying to take from us, some victory he is attempting to stop.** Something God wants to give us in our situation that the enemy is trying to steal.

I don't think I have ever been more fearful about illness than I was after suffering the stroke in 2012. I never knew a stroke affected a person in so many different ways! All my life, I had been fiercely independent. I had had to be, living on my own for so many years, with children to feed. I had never been disabled in any way before, even though I suffered terrible back pain for decades.

Day after day, I struggled to do small everyday tasks, yet there was almost nothing I could do for myself at first. Even two months later, there were still many tasks I could not perform without assistance.

Having never been unable to take care of myself before, I was not only frustrated, I was terrified. Terrified my abilities might not return soon, terrified I would be left disabled and alone.

As I continually reminded myself of the Lord's words to me, my fear eventually left. I knew He had already told me He would restore me, though I sometimes feared it might be years before it happened because I was really struggling to see myself well in the face of all the doctor's reports, not to mention the many medications I now took every day. In the meantime, to fight the fear, I decided to work on what I could. I would start with trying to see myself well.

There are many factors that affect how we see ourselves after an illness or major life event like the stroke I had: our pain level, our perception of the illness and possible chance of recovery, our loved ones' perceptions of our state of health, our doctors' reports, and what we believe about God's Word regarding our illness.

It is very difficult to see yourself well while your body is wracked with pain. Having degeneration in my spine, it had been so many years since I had been pain free, that I couldn't remember when the last time was. I thought it was around the time I was 18.

It was a challenge to try to think radiant health while constantly taking medicines and consulting doctors. I knew I would have to fight for a new self image, to somehow see myself able and well in my mind while shuffling around on a walker, but I knew being fully healed would be worth it if I could do it. And I knew **God never asks His people to do anything He does not also empower them to do.**

The wonderful thing about healing through God's Word (well, *one* of the wonderful things!) is that once you master it, you can be well from that day forward – for the rest of your life.

Over and over each day, the enemy presented me with mental images of myself still hobbling around, disabled, still having to hire help years into the future. He knew I had no way to pay for that kind of help. I was already struggling. I determined that was one place I would have to fight to replace those images with a picture of what the Lord had told me - 100% function restored.

One morning as I lay in bed, despair filled my mind. I was improving so slowly that I was afraid it would take a year or more to even see much improvement in my abilities. That would mean I couldn't write the books, or maybe even do any radio programs. I was nearly helpless, having to hire help for even the simplest activities. On top of that, the ministry provided all my income. I had no other way to provide for myself, having already given up my career in Oil & Gas research. God had told me not to work, that He would provide for me, and I had obeyed and left my job. What if I could not work the ministry? How would I live? I certainly was not able to work a regular job now.

I tried to pull myself out from under the dark cloud of despair, with no success. Everything felt so hopeless.

A couple of months after the stroke, my son moved out to a place he had bought. Though I missed his conversation, I was so glad for him, it was the fulfillment of a long-held dream. He wanted his own place, and now he finally had it. Being completely alone with so many things I could not do for myself made me fearful, but I soon hired an out of work friend to help me with housework, grocery shopping and driving me to doctor visits.

In an attempt to distract myself from the hopelessness trying to overwhelm me, I began to pray about moving from the small, dreary rent house where I had lived for almost four years. When God confirmed I was released, I was so happy! If I hadn't been on a walker when He told me, I would have broken into my Happy Dance! I would finally get to move out of that dark, dreary little house that had come to feel like a prison!

Even though I was recovering from the stroke, and I had no idea how on earth I could possibly pack, move and unpack, I didn't want to waste any time moving out. Some friends helped me find a larger place, and when God confirmed that place was His will for me, I paid them to help me pack up and move to it.

Even though I couldn't do much of the work besides packing and a little cleaning, the move was still exhausting because of the million small decisions I had to make and all the utility connect/disconnects, the mail forwarding, and other moving details I had to deal with, but even so, within a couple of weeks, I was in new surroundings.

Many nights - sometimes every night for a week straight - I would awaken at two or three a.m., terrified and shaking, as the enemy flooded my mind with fearful thoughts of never getting better, and even of getting worse - of falling down the steep staircase at my new place, of having another stroke while living alone. I would lay awake for hours, terrified and unable to go back to sleep.

One night I awoke terrified and fighting back tears. I felt so afraid and so alone. So I began praying, and poured out my heart to God, as I always did.

Please help me, Lord. I am so afraid of being disabled, and I feel so afraid of being alone right now! Please help me get through this and get well again. And please comfort me so I won't feel so afraid. I know this fear is not from You!

I had rebuked the fear spirit night after night, but it persisted and since I was no longer under the Curse of Fear, having broken it when I lived at the old house, I wasn't sure why.

Just then I felt God's comforting presence wrap around me like a warm, soft blanket. The fear could not stand in His presence, and it dissipated completely, as I felt His love and peace wrap around me. I relaxed in His embrace and fell back to sleep, a smile on my face. I knew everything was going to be alright, I just didn't know for sure when.

I had not lived in a house with a staircase since I was a teenager and right after the stroke seemed like the worst possible time, but I loved the townhouse otherwise. Each day when I had to go up the stairs, I would cling to the one rail on the left for dear life and pray not to lose my balance. Several times I did teeter on the top step, and feel like I was going to fall backwards, but suddenly I would stabilize and be okay. Going down the stairs was even more terrifying. It was a daily struggle just to get up and down that staircase when even walking was a chore, but I was determined.

One evening I was praying at bedtime right after having climbed up the stairs again.

Lord, please help me keep my balance on those stairs, I'm so afraid I might fall and have another stroke! No one would even find me for weeks here because I don't know anyone! You are my only friend here until I make some more. Please help me, Lord!

The Lord showed me something then in my spirit I will never forget. He showed me a big angel with beautiful white wings sitting on the staircase. He showed me that was why I hadn't fallen all the times I had teetered on the top landing and felt like I was going to fall backwards or forwards. He had assigned an angel to help me up and down those stairs so I would never fall! What a merciful and loving God we serve!

I knew then I didn't have to be afraid on those stairs ever again.

One day a few weeks later about midday, I was hobbling about and I began thinking about how slowly my recovery seemed to be going. I feared being disabled and alone. I had no money to hire anyone to help me with anything now, having spent the last of my small savings on the move. I had not been able to pay the hospital bills I had incurred with the stroke, and that grieved me greatly. Having lived in poverty for so much of my life, I hated owing money I could not pay.

The last week's hospital stay was donated and I had written a thank you note to the rehab hospital in Allen for their kindness, but I owed all the doctors and for all the lab tests, etc. and for the first two weeks at McKinney Medical Center which, without insurance, were exorbitant. I prayed I would someday be able to pay them. I had called and tried to work out payment plans but the hospital wanted over $500 a month and I could not pay that. I didn't know what to do but pray. They had reduced what I owed drastically, but I still owed about $20,000 altogether and I had no hope of ever having that kind of money to pay all those bills. All I could do was ask the Lord to help me someday to be able to pay them.

The combination of owing so much debt, when I tried so hard not to owe anything more than a vehicle payment or other really necessary expense, and the disabilities in my body that I faced every day were really taking a toll on my mental state and I was fighting the depression and severe fatigue that all stroke victims face. I was fighting it but losing the battle. I was still so weak, there was very little fight anywhere in me.

As I felt the familiar spirit of fear began to creep up on me and the feeling of hopelessness crushing down on me, I began to pray.

Lord, there are so many things facing me right now I don't know where to start. This fear is terrible, and it keeps coming back even after I rebuke it. Please show me what to do.

A minute or two later, I was reminded of a vision I had had many years before and had forgotten about for a long time. I called it the Word of God vision.

One night during prayer around the end of October of 1999, in a vision I saw a line of doors, each having a label on it. Some of the doors I saw were sickness, poverty, depression and debt. Then I saw a mountain of a man, big and burly looking, with huge muscles bulging out everywhere, with a huge jutting chest and powerful legs. I watched as he crashed through each door one by one, without so much as lifting his hand to push on it.

Immediately after the last one, he looked around with a look on his face as if to say, 'Where's the challenge?' He was so strong, nothing seemed to be even the slightest challenge to him. Then he turned towards me and I saw his shirt. On it were the words 'Power of God.'

What does this mean, Lord? How can I use that power?

Then the Lord showed me my faith in the spirit mixing with His Word - the man walked towards me, then he walked right into my body, and became a part of me. Next I saw the muscle man (that power) start operating through me. The Lord showed me that if I would learn His Word, and mix my faith with it, the enemy's tactics would have no power against me.

Jeremiah 33:3

Call unto me, and I will answer thee, and show thee great and mighty things, which thou knowest not.

As the Word says in Jeremiah 33:3, if we call upon the Lord, He will answer us and show us what we do not know. It was a simple truth, and surely one I knew in my head, but now I had more true understanding of how it could work – for me.

So often we see God's power working in others, and the enemy will try to convince us it will work for *them*, but not for *us*. We aren't worthy, God doesn't like us, we're not good enough, blah, blah, blah. It's all a pack of lies. We *are* worthy because of what Jesus did for us.

God is no respecter of persons, He is a respecter of *faith*. He is a respecter of *His Word*. He is a respecter of the sacrifice of our Lord Jesus.

Flipping my Bible open to Psalms, I sat down in my rocking chair and began reading out loud every beautiful passage of promise I could find that I had highlighted, to remind me of God's beautiful promises in my life. I might not see every promise happening just then, but I knew they were all true just the same. I proceeded through Psalms and read each one out loud, thinking about how wonderful and merciful God is to give His children so much.

About half an hour later, I finished and closed my Bible. A great cloud of peace now settled around me. God's Word had worked yet again.

I was thrilled to realize I could access His peace any time I needed it that way.

Fear would never be able to beat me now!

Over the next months as I struggled to recover in my new place, I adopted two rescue dogs to keep me company. They helped to dispel much of the loneliness and depression I was suffering and gave me yet another reason to get up each day.

Getting better and better

I was steadily improving, working on the books, doing the ministry again, and making friends in my new neighborhood. Late in 2013, I decided to take a trip at Christmas, something I seldom ever did. I returned home to Princeton in early January 2014 after a long holiday stay for the first time since the stroke had happened over a year earlier. The drive each way in the seemingly never-ending winter storms of 2013-14 was brutally tiring but flying made me ill and I couldn't navigate airports, so it just had to be endured. I felt the weather reporters had accurately named that winter:

Snowmagedon. I usually enjoyed the few times a year I saw snow in Texas, but I came home from that trip hating it.

The next evening after arriving back home, I laid down on the couch to take a rest and when I awoke, I felt overheated and nauseous.

Really nauseous. It felt like I awoke with a big V for Virus running through my bloodstream.

I jumped up and ran for the bathroom nearby but determined on the way I would not give in to it regardless. In the restroom, I began rebuking the nausea and any sickness that was behind it in the Name of Jesus, telling my body it was healed by the stripes of Jesus. Within minutes the nausea receded and I felt normal.

I was thrilled that the Blood of Jesus had won yet another victory over the enemy. This meant I didn't have to give in to another virus ever!

Not long after, I began confessing more boldly that I was healed and 100% restored from the stroke. I wanted complete, radiant health and nothing less, and I knew from what God had told me that I could have it if I was willing to fight for it and fight hard.

I was.

One evening in late February when I had not been feeling especially well, I again began to feel the tell-tale symptoms of a virus attacking my body. It was attacking hard and fast and I immediately began praying for strength.

Please help, Lord! I don't have the strength or time to deal with a virus. Please don't let this be a virus I'm feeling! Please strengthen me against whatever this is!

If you fight it, you'll win.

That was all I needed to hear. The fight was on.

Glynda Lomax

I began rebuking every virus symptom and the virus itself in the Name of Jesus. I declared I was healed by the stripes of Jesus, over and over. In less than an hour, all the symptoms left my body.

God had won another victory!

One morning not long after that, I awoke with pain in my left hip. I had felt it before, especially early in the mornings, and it usually left after a little while, so I proceeded with getting up and going about my morning routine.

As I took my dogs out for a walk, I noticed the pain did not leave but instead grew worse, so I cut the walk short and returned home.

I rebuked the pain and told Satan I was healed by the stripes of Jesus and to back off. Not one to run to a doctor at the first sign of trouble, I planned to do everything I could to avoid going.

Whenever I climbed the stairs I noticed the pain grew much worse. As I sat down and ice packed the hip, I knew I would not be able to put off going to the doctor long. The pain level was startling. By the next day, the pain grew so intense I was shaking and gritting my teeth trying to bear it and the only thing that helped it was to ice pack it and sit very still.

It was Thursday and I worked on the radio show all day, hoping the pain would subside so I could record it, but it grew steadily worse. I knew I would just have to push through it the best I could, which I did. As soon as the show was aired, I headed for bed. Friday I awoke fine, but like on Thursday, as soon as I walked downstairs, I was in agonizing pain that grew with every step.

I got ready and went to see a doctor at my favorite walk-in clinic. By the time I arrived there, I was shaking and gritting my teeth with the pain again and the wait felt like an eternity, although I'm sure it was only minutes. The doctor x-rayed my hip to be sure nothing was broken. It was a flare-up of bursitis, which I had experienced before but always forgot as soon as it stopped hurting.

She gave me a strong injection of two steroids and sent me home with a prescription for strong oral steroids as well. When the pain did not get better that afternoon, I called and she told me I could start the oral steroids early. I finally gave up and went to bed early with my ice pack, since nothing else seemed to be helping. I scolded myself for not fighting it spiritually and demanding my right to health and freedom from pain. The pain had taken over all my thoughts when it became severe so fast and I had simply forgotten my right to healing.

I would have to try harder.

I wondered as I tried to find a comfortable position on the ice pack if the Lord was not going to allow the steroids to work to remind me to fight the battle the proper way. That would grieve me, not only because the pain was hindering my activities so much, but also because of the cost of the doctor visit.

The next morning the pain began before I was even completely sitting up on the edge of the bed. I knew the enemy was trying to set me up for a miserable day. I also knew I could not let the pain stop me from doing what needed to be done. Satan had no right to put that pain on me and I was determined to send it back to him and to hell, for all eternity.

I made my way downstairs slowly and painfully, made coffee and sat down with my ice pack. A garbage truck picking up garbage across the street reminded me I didn't have to let Satan dump his trash on me anymore.

I began to do battle.

"In the Name of Jesus, I command all the inflammation and pain in this hip to leave and go immediately into the Abyss. I rebuke this bursitis in Jesus Name. I am a child of the Most High God and you have no right to put sickness on me, Satan – I command you to take it off right now in Jesus Name!"

Then I grabbed my Bible and opened it to Isaiah and I began going through the tabbies where I had marked all the healing scriptures, and I began praying them out loud, personalizing each one to make it a confession of personal healing.

"Surely He has borne **my** griefs and carried **my** sorrows; yet we did esteem him stricken and smitten of God, and afflicted; But He was wounded for **my** transgressions, He was bruised for **my** iniquities; the chastisement of **my** peace was upon Him; and with His stripes **I AM healed!**"

"No weapon that is formed against **me** shall prosper, and every tongue that shall rise against **me** in judgment, **I** shall condemn!"

Satan declaring you ill, demons declaring you ill or in pain or having a disease – these are all tongues rising against you in judgment. The tongues of devils.

As I continued through my morning, I continued to rebuke the inflammation, and the pain in the Name of Jesus. I told my hip it was healed in the Name of Jesus and commanded the bursitis to leave my body.

It is important to know when you begin a battle for your healing that whatever is wrong will seldom leave just with one rebuke, although occasionally with huge faith that is without any doubt, I *have* seen that happen with more minor afflictions, such as the sinus infection I had several years ago that my friend Katrina E. rebuked in a single phone call. She spoke with faith and the authority of a true believer and shut that infection down completely!

How long it takes to manifest healing can be linked to how long you have been receiving and entertaining whatever is wrong. This time I was three days in on suffering severe pain and immobility. Now I had to battle the inflammation and pain that I had allowed to take root – but I was willing to – for however long it took, so I could be free of it once and for all.

By early June, I was having the hip pain less frequently, but it was likely due to staying still as much as possible. I could tell I had gained ten or so pounds, but when moving around is so incredibly

Glynda Lomax

painful, you don't care much about that. I found that using a walker around the house also helped to take some of the strain off the hip and made moving around a little more bearable.

Lord, I'm so tired of fighting this! I honestly just wish I could sit in my rocker and grow old quietly, while working on quilts or something. I think life has worn me out.

It was so much easier to just give in to the pain than it was to keep doing battle all the time. I would get pain, then get tired from the pain and not want to fight any more. I suspected everyone who dealt with chronic pain probably felt this way at one time or another. There were so many days when the pain felt much bigger than I felt. And maybe it was.

But it *wasn't* bigger than God and I wasn't going to just give up because being in pain would not glorify Him!

When we are especially weary, it is easier for illness to get to us, and harder to remember at first that it has no right to. If you have spent years submitting to every pain and illness like I did, it may take a little while to remember to battle every time, like it did for me.

Be patient with yourself as your faith and spiritual warfare strength ramp up. They will. The more we use our spiritual muscles, the stronger they become and if you don't give up, you will develop a faith that can deal a quick and deadly blow to the enemy every time. The key is to keep your mind stayed on the Word of God. Then when you need it, it will be abiding in you, and it will rise up and answer the sickness or pain *for* you, at the same time reminding you that they are not yours and you don't have to keep them.

PRAISE DANCE

I am of the charismatic faith, and I believe in all the gifts of the spirit, but I have often felt uncomfortable being bold and open with my worship in a corporate environment with a body of believers.

On a summer weekend in 2007, I was at a women's spiritual warfare conference in Oklahoma, which was being hosted by the couple who ordained me. A song began to play, that I later began calling the "Rain Dance Song" because it sang about a rain dance. It was a Christian song, of course. All the ladies in the room began to dance around the room in worship to the Lord. I was sitting in my chair, being my usual reserved and quiet little self when the Lord spoke to me.

The people who are up dancing are getting things broken off of them!

I still had many struggles I needed God's help with and when He said that, I practically leapt off my chair and began to follow the other women around and dance! Joy filled me as I worshipped the Lord with them.

It is important we join in when worship is happening, both on the inside of us and the outside. If you are not very demonstrative in public like me, just do what you can. The Lord wants to bless you as you worship and He will help you.

Later in 2007, I was on a job in Northwestern Oklahoma, standing at my mirror doing a quick makeup before going to the courthouse to do research one morning when the Lord spoke something to me. I had loved tanning since I was in my 30's, and frequented tanning beds every summer. I actually did it more for the intense relaxation it provided than for the tan. It was like a 20 minute vacation every evening that felt like a soft cloud of quiet warmth on a sunny beach somewhere.

I cannot protect you from skin cancer if you continue tanning.

That was all He said. But that was all He needed to say. I went to the phone and canceled every tanning appointment I had and I have never made another one since then.

Glynda Lomax

Though our God is mighty to heal, we must use wisdom in how we treat our bodies. We cannot eat five candy bars a day for twenty years and expect we will not become obese and diabetic. God can heal the diabetes, but if we continue to abuse our bodies, we will cause it again.

It is imperative if we want to be well that we also do anything He tells us or leads us to do. Anything He speaks to us or leads us to do is always for our own good.

There are many diseases that are caused by our own abuse and sinful habits, and we must do our part if we want to be healed and stay healed of those.

I will be the first to admit I don't eat a perfect diet, but what you do most of the time matters far more than what you do once in awhile. I don't work out at a gym every day like when I was younger, but I do walk every day that I possibly can.

At 54, I don't need perfectly sculpted muscles or a weight lifter's body, but I do need good cardiovascular health. I do need clarity in my mind, not the fogginess that takes over with a sedentary lifestyle and a bad diet. Exercise doesn't have to be hard, but our bodies were made to move, not sit still in front of our computers and television sets all the time. Everyone is able to do something.

Eating healthy doesn't have to be impossible, either. I don't have to eat perfectly, if I just make the healthy choices most of the time, my mostly healthy diet will cover me for the other times when I am eating less than healthy.

In the Bible, we see many examples of healing being linked to forgiveness. In 1997, I had been in this walk for about a year and a half when one night I was reading the Word, and I came across Matthew 6:14-15.

Matthew 6:14-15

For if ye forgive men their trespasses, your heavenly Father will also forgive you: But if ye forgive not men their trespasses, neither will your Father forgive your trespasses.

When I read that I would not be forgiven if I did not forgive others, I panicked. I was not willing to go to hell for *anyone*, no matter what they had done to me! I immediately made a list of all the people I felt I had unforgiveness towards, including, of course, my abusive ex-husband.

I got down on my knees and went down the list, confessing to the Lord my unforgiveness and asking for forgiveness and help forgiving, doing my best to release each instance to the Lord. I saved my ex-husband for last, as I knew he would be the most difficult to forgive. When I didn't feel I could do it, that I could let go of all the pain and anger, I became really afraid.

Lord, please help me! I don't know how to forgive Rick for all those miserable years and I am not willing to go to hell over that. I am not getting up out of this floor until You help me forgive him – I can't take the chance I could die suddenly and have unforgiveness!

I continued crying out to the Lord until, about five minutes later, I felt a touch from heaven. Suddenly my spirit was flooded with visions of many terrible things my ex-husband had suffered as a child, and the Lord filled me with compassion for him. For the first time since our divorce, I was genuinely able to pray for him to be saved and blessed with all my heart and soul, and I continued to do so from that night forward.

Most of the memories of the abuse left me in that moment. What little I still remembered afterwards, I felt no emotion about. All the anger, and all the pain, was completely gone. The torment of all those years was finally over! **Forgiveness has the power to heal.**

Matthew 18:34-35

And his lord was wroth, and delivered him to the tormentors, till he should pay all that was due unto him. So likewise shall my heavenly Father do also unto you, if ye from your hearts forgive not every one his brother their trespasses.

Just months later, the Lord had taken me out of oilfield work and I was living in a tiny house in Sayre, Oklahoma waiting for the Lord to tell me what was next. One of the ladies I sang with at church, came to my house one morning and casually said, "Hey, I was praying for you this morning and the Lord told me to tell you He has healed all the emotional effects of your marriage."

My friend Beverly B., who brought me the message, did not know I had been diagnosed with Post Traumatic Stress Disorder (PTSD) in the early 1990's, and that I had suffered years of terrible nightmares and full blown flashbacks of the abuse after leaving my husband Rick in 1987.

It was all I could do not to jump up and break into my Happy Dance! He had set me free from those awful nightmares and flashbacks!

I was Free!

He had sent His Word and healed me!

Psalm 107:20

He sent his word, and healed them, and delivered them from their destructions.

Unforgiveness holds the door open to the pain of the past. It is the stiff, unyielding hand that clings to what someone did to *us*. Unforgiveness is all about *us*.

This is especially true regarding PTSD – Post Traumatic Stress Disorder is directly related to unforgiveness. Sometimes it is ourselves we must forgive. Sometimes it is our abuser, or a person in authority over us. Sometimes it is even God, if we are blaming Him for something that happened (or didn't happen). Sometimes, like in Matthew 9, we need our sins forgiven so we can receive our healing; sometimes we need to forgive others.

Matthew 9

2 And, behold, they brought to him a man sick of the palsy, lying on a bed: and Jesus seeing their faith said unto the sick of the palsy; Son, be of good cheer; thy sins be forgiven thee.

3 And, behold, certain of the scribes said within themselves, This man blasphemeth.

4 And Jesus knowing their thoughts said, Wherefore think ye evil in your hearts?

5 For whether is easier, to say, Thy sins be forgiven thee; or to say, Arise, and walk?

6 But that ye may know that the Son of man hath power on earth to forgive sins, (then saith he to the sick of the palsy,) Arise, take up thy bed, and go unto thine house.

7 And he arose, and departed to his house.

8 But when the multitudes saw it, they marvelled, and glorified God, which had given such power unto men.

God is always glorified when His children forgive others who have wronged them, and when we make amends with others and ask for their forgiveness when we have wronged them.

DELIVERANCE CAN BRING HEALING

Sometimes, as Jesus shows us through His ministry, healing comes by way of deliverance from demonic influences.

Back in about 2000, my friend T. Winchester drove me to South Dallas to pray for a sweet woman who had been totally disabled for eight years. She was a Christian, but suffered horribly from some type of arthritis that caused her to not be able to walk normally for about two hours after she got up each morning. After we talked for awhile, I told her I was ready to pray for her. She stood before me and as I laid my hands on her, the Lord spoke clearly to me.

It's a Spirit of Infirmity. Cast it out!

I had little experience with spiritual warfare at that point in my walk, but did as I was told. My whole prayer over her lasted maybe 30 seconds, as I cast out the spirit in Jesus' Name and asked for the Lord's blessing on her and her household.

Three days later, she was completely healed and the next week, T. called to tell me the woman had gone to work for her church full time! Our God is awesome to heal those who dare to believe Him as she did.

CURSED OBJECTS HINDER HEALING

Once, I was watching a program on television and saw an older man who had cancer in multiple areas of his body. I felt compassion for him, and for his family, who did not want him to die, and I began praying for his healing. Then the Lord spoke to me.

He has accursed objects in his house, I can't answer your prayer, or anyone's prayers for him unless he gets rid of those and repents for owning them.

Deuteronomy 7:26

Neither shalt thou bring an abomination into thine house, lest thou be a cursed thing like it: but thou shalt utterly detest it, and thou shalt utterly abhor it; for it is a cursed thing.

OTHER HINDRANCES TO HEALING

Most healings are progressive, though we do occasionally still see the miraculous sudden healings the Bible talks about. No one knows for sure why everyone does not receive an immediate miracle. There are generational curses that can cause illness – the Witchcraft Curse causes all manner of mental disorders. The Curse of Infirmity causes frequent infections, and also causes many illnesses that have no definitive diagnosis. This spirit is known to move around in the body, and it also causes moral weakness. Any person with a Spirit of Infirmity will have a terrible time trying to walk in holiness until they break this curse off their life.

THE PROVERBS 17:13 CURSE – SIN AND CONSEQUENCES

Another cause the Lord showed me of people not getting healed is what I call the Proverbs 17:13 curse:

Proverbs 17:13

Whoso rewardeth evil for good, evil shall not depart from his house.

Whenever someone returns evil on someone who has done them only good, a curse comes on their house and destruction will not depart from it from then on. This is a spiritual law. This happened to King David when he caused Uriah the Hittite's death so he could have Bathsheba, Uriah's wife. From then on, destruction never departed from David's house, even though King David confessed he had sinned and repented to the Prophet Nathan, who brought him the news:

2 Samuel 12:9-14

9 Wherefore hast thou despised the commandment of the Lord, to do evil in his sight? thou hast killed Uriah the Hittite with the sword, and hast taken his wife to be thy wife, and hast slain him with the sword of the children of Ammon.

10 Now therefore the sword shall never depart from thine house; because thou hast despised me, and hast taken the wife of Uriah the Hittite to be thy wife.

11 Thus saith the Lord, Behold, I will raise up evil against thee out of thine own house, and I will take thy wives before thine eyes, and give them unto thy neighbour, and he shall lie with thy wives in the sight of this sun.

12 For thou didst it secretly: but I will do this thing before all Israel, and before the sun.

13 And David said unto Nathan, I have sinned against the Lord. And Nathan said unto David, The Lord also hath put away thy sin; thou shalt not die.

14 Howbeit, because by this deed thou hast given great occasion to the enemies of the Lord to blaspheme, the child also that is born unto thee shall surely die.

There are often still consequences even after we repent of a sin. Let's say a teenage couple commits fornication and she becomes pregnant. They repent of their sin.

But she is still pregnant, isn't she? So we can be forgiven but still have consequences of our sins.

I continued to fight for my healing, occasionally still forgetting I was healed, until at last I got the mindset that does not allow any symptom to arrive unchecked. Or unrebuked.

It was late in September of 2014, and I was talking to a friend about what each of us were writing.

I was still working on *The Healing Companion*, the second of the Companion Series the Lord had assigned me to write.

"What do you not have for the book?" he asked.

"I don't have the ending. I can't end the book unless I am completely, totally healed. How can I tell anyone else how to get healed unless I first got healed myself?" I said.

"What about you is not healed yet?" he asked, simply.

I was silent. Thinking, searching.

"You're healed," he said. "So finish the book."

I was speechless. There was no sickness or pain in my body, but I was still on prescription medication for the aftereffects of that deadly stroke.

For so long, I had lived with so much pain that I had become accustomed to it. Almost expectant.

I became so busy looking at and for the things that were wrong that I was missing what was right. Right there in front of me, right there inside of me.

He chose us in Him before the creation of the world and came up with a plan before we even existed. He gave to us resurrection power through Jesus Christ, our Lord.

A power that is inside of all of us.

But it is all too often weakened by all the things outside us. The truth, however, is that we were healed long before we were ever hurt. Long before we ever had one single symptom, He healed us.

....greater is He that is in me, than he that is in the world. (1 John 4:4)

After we got off the phone that day, I could not stop thinking about that one simple question. I love the way he stated that in such simple terms, and left me thinking about it for hours, even days.

What about you is not healed yet?

That evening after our phone call, I got a phone call from my regular doctor, the one who monitored my medications. She had never called me personally before. The results of my most recent bloodwork showed the cholesterol medication she had me on was affecting my liver. She wanted me to discontinue it immediately. I felt that was another confirmation. Healed people don't need medication. My blood pressure had tested dangerously low on two of my last three visits to her. She had reduced it from the original four times a day to now only one time a day. How exciting to see so much evidence of my healing in one day!

That night, I also discontinued another medication I had taken the whole two years since the stroke, one that helped with the nerve pain in my left side. Though I no longer had paralysis in my left side, I had been left with large areas of nerve pain that felt like burning needles all the way down my left arm, left leg and my left foot. The medication kept it bearable, but I knew I was healed. I no longer wanted to take medications. Two drugs down, two more to go. The following week, I stopped taking another one. In an effort to walk in wisdom and not get the cart before the horse, I would get my doctor's okay before coming off the last blood pressure pill, but I knew the Lord would show her I no longer needed that one, either, at my next appointment. It would be foolhardy to stop the blood pressure medicine after blood pressure caused that stroke.

The medication did not matter to me, I knew – REALLY KNEW – I was already healed.

I had worked towards manifesting my full healing long enough to know not every symptom had to line up for me to *be* healed, though we often expect that before we *believe* we are healed.

The bottom line was, God's Word said I was healed, and there was no authority anywhere in the world that was higher than His truth. God had shown me again and again that healing was mine, it was time I claimed it once and for all and walked in it.

And that meant I could walk in divine health for the rest of my life!

I never suffered any side effects of coming off my medications, and the enemy has not succeeded with any of his further attempts to make me ill. I continue to stand on the powerful Word of God and claim my healing, sending every other symptom back to hell, where it belongs.

NOTE: Please do not stop taking life-saving medications without knowing for sure you have heard from the Lord. This is not something to take lightly. The medications I stopped were more for comfort, and I only stopped them after knowing He was showing me in my spirit that I no longer needed them because He had already healed me. One of my relatives was diagnosed with high blood pressure and refused to take the blood pressure medicine prescribed, suffered a crippling, life-changing stroke and is now in hospice care. As I update this book in 2019, I still take the one small dose of blood pressure medicine each day. I prayed about stopping it, but the Lord never okayed it. I could not get my doctors to okay it. Do NOT stop life-saving medicines. This for me did not interfere with me receiving my healing. If taking that one pill made me feel I was still unwell, it might be different, but it doesn't.

*KNOW THAT as you fight for your healing, the attacks will increase. This is not an increase in sickness, but an increase in symptoms designed to make you back down.

Attack harder, stand stronger and praise louder when it happens. The enemy knows beyond any shadow of a doubt that if you continue to press in, you *will* be healed. He is trying to scare you into stopping. He is trying to convince you that *your* illness is too severe or that God may heal everyone else, but He won't heal *you*. He tried that with me, too. He has tried it with everyone for centuries who has pressed in for healing. Don't buy the lie.

* KNOW THAT you must fight hardest when you least feel like fighting. I fought when I felt sick, when the pain was so bad that all I really wanted to do was crawl into bed and give up, when I was so tired I could hardly stay awake, and when my eyes were filled with tears because the pain was so overwhelming. I fought when the doctors told me nothing could be done except pain pills. I fought when I was too busy, too exhausted, and when I felt like it was hopeless. You will too if you want to claim what is yours.

* KNOW THAT people around you will look at you like you're crazy, that they will tell you that you just need to accept the illness and make the best of it. Don't buy the world's facts when God is offering you the truth of His healing.

The enemy will attack through others as much as he attacks you directly. He will use other people to speak sickness and disease to you, especially if he can't get you to speak it.

Know these attacks will come and start early shutting them out. Many more people would get healed if it weren't for all the people around them telling them how ill they are. You must listen only to what God's Word says about you. It says you have already been healed.

* KNOW THAT healing can and usually does take time. Dodie Osteen, who is well known for having been miraculously healed of late stage liver cancer, fought for six long, pain filled months to receive hers, but the alternative was to lay down and die in two weeks. It's your choice.

DO'S AND DONT'S FOR HEALING

1. You must desire your healing enough that you are willing to fight and not back down for however long it is going to take. Do not start this until you are ready for a fight because the enemy will increase his attack against you as soon as he sees you are determined to be healed, and if you're not willing to fight, you will only end up in more pain.

2. You must understand - and have your own personal revelation (not mine, not Kenneth Hagin's, not anyone else's) - that it is truly God's will for you to be WELL, not sick. You are not suffering for the glory of God - He doesn't get any glory from that. God gets glory from you being well and healed and fully functioning. If you have any doubt at all about that, you are double minded and will waver and you won't receive your healing. Study healing until you know that you know that you know you are supposed to be healed.

3. You must have revelation that healing is truly part of you right under the atonement. That you have an absolute RIGHT to be healed under the work Jesus did on the cross. If you don't know this is your absolute right, the devil will be able to convince you to give up the fight. He will increase your symptoms and tell you why you SHOULD be sick and in pain, and in the dark of a painful night, you may start believing him.

Do a word study using a Strong's Exhaustive Concordance on the word salvation in the New Testament. When you see the definition of the word translated salvation, you will see the atonement gave you the right to be healed absolutely. That means you have just as much right to healing as you do to salvation when you believe in Jesus.

4. You must decide you are not willing to accept some illnesses and pains and not others. Otherwise, the enemy will only attack you in some other area. He will let you have healing in one area and begin attacking you in all the places you find sickness and pain "acceptable." You have the absolute right to TOTAL HEALING AND WELLNESS. You're either healed or you're not. Which is it?

* A recording of the healing scriptures that speak to your spirit for listening to whenever possible can be very helpful.

* It may seem like standing for healing is demanding something from God. It isn't. If I buy you an airline ticket and it's at the counter waiting for you to pick it up, are you demanding something from the airline clerk when you go to claim it? No, you are simply claiming what is **already yours**. Healing is the same.

* Make up your own list of healing scriptures. Choose the ones that speak loudest to your spirit about your healing. When I suffered through an excruciating bout of sciatica in 2010, I came across a scripture in Nahum that said "this affliction will not arise a second time. It was not even about sickness or disease, but it spoke loudly to my spirit. I knew sciatica not only could last for years, but was known to reoccur over and over, and I decided to declare that scripture even as I was suffering, and forbid it to return, even if I didn't know how to get healed from it at time.

Nahum 1:9

What do ye imagine against the LORD? he will make an utter end: affliction shall not rise up the second time.

I began quoting that the affliction would not arise a second time, even when the pain was so bad I was almost in tears. Over and over I said it. The following year in 2011, it did try to return. I began quoting the scripture again, and it went away without ever fully manifesting. It is 2019 as I update this book and sciatica has **never** come back again. God's Word has power, period. If a scripture speaks to you about your healing, use it. Don't worry about the context if your spirit bears witness with it. There is life in His Word!

* Set aside the time necessary to make your healing your sole focus, even if it's just a weekend, if at all possible. This may be difficult if you have family responsibilities, but it will help you receive far more quickly if you can do it. Otherwise, your healing fight will be hit and miss, and your healing manifestation will be, too. And like the old saying says, "A stitch in time saves nine." A little work towards healing now can save you months or even years of illness later.

* Don't let your circumstances steal your praise. The Israelites did this at the waters of Marah. Just before that in Exodus 15, they were singing a song of praise and worship to the Lord for the great victory He had wrought for them. Then they came to the water, and it was bitter, and immediately they began murmuring and complaining against Moses. Blaming doesn't help you, it only holds you back. The word for complain in this story in the Bible actually means "Remain" so if you complain, you will remain right where you are.

* Put yourself in the enemy's place. If you were him, and you were trying to stop you from manifesting your healing, how would you attack you? Make a list of how the enemy is likely to attack the healing process - he will increase the pain, attack you again and again to wear you down, and he'll tell you how awful you feel to try to make you go to bed instead of going to battle. Maybe he sees you listen to the opinions of your family above all else, in which case he may attack your healing through them.

He'll add other sicknesses to your list of ailments to weaken you and try to keep you from fighting. He'll attack you with self-pity to take the fight out of you.

He'll do everything possible to distract you from studying to get revelation on healing or make you too busy to work on your healing. He doesn't need to get you into sin to get your focus off healing, he only needs to get your thoughts all wrapped up in something else.

He'll try to tell you that you're doing it wrong or it isn't working, or that it works for other people, but not you. He'll suggest medical treatment instead of attacking healing. For me it was the chiropractor, which had helped me many years before - I knew it wouldn't work - God won't let other things solve your problem when He's trying to get a revelation to you, I was looking for a quick fix so I could keep up with my schedule. All it did was deplete my bank account, take up my time, and leave me frustrated. Years ago, it worked a lot better).

He'll tell you God is a terrible god for letting you suffer so badly. He knows if you become angry at God, you'll lose your faith and he can steal your praise. Angry, bitter people don't work on receiving healing by faith. They wallow in their anger.

He'll tell you that everyone around you will think you're strange, or crazy, when you start rebuking the enemy out loud and claiming your healing. This may actually happen, but you must die to it so you can move forward. Which do you want? A positive opinion by people, or to be healed?

He'll use his favorite line "What are you going to do if...... (the pain never ends, you can't work, it gets worse, fill in the blank)??? to try to get you into fear and doubt and worry.

He will try hard to get you into fear, like he did me. Fear has a way of taking over all your thoughts and sapping all your energy.

I always believed if the doctor ever told me I had cancer that I would stand strong and courageous against the diagnosis, because I had always confessed I would never get it, in spite of the fact that both of my parents had it. Even when I had a tumor removed in the early eighties, I hadn't been afraid. It was benign, but I never doubted it would be, in spite of the fact it was growing rapidly.

But I will never as long as I live forget what I felt when, back around 2002 or 2003, my doctor who was performing a sonogram got a certain look on her face and told me I had two growths that appeared to be tumors, just inside my uterus.

My Mother had had uterine cancer.

Fear surged through my mind and body before my mind had time to stop it, and I almost panicked. It is so easy to get into fear when we get a bad report. We go to our doctors, who are the authorities in the world of medicine and healing, so they can fix us. They are the experts, right?

Wrong.

The number 1 expert on how to fix anything is always, always, always the original creator. And in the case of our bodies, that's our God.

2 Timothy 1:7

For God hath not given us the spirit of fear; but ot power, and of love, and of a sound mind.

Isaiah 41:10

Fear thou not; for I am with thee: be not dismayed; for I am thy God: I will strengthen thee; yea, I will help thee; yea, I will uphold thee with the right hand of my righteousness.

Isaiah 54:17 - No weapon that is formed against thee shall prosper; and every tongue that shall rise against thee in judgment thou shalt condemn. This is the heritage of the servants of the Lord, and their righteousness is of me, saith the Lord.

I John 4:4 - Ye are of God, little children, and have overcome them: because greater is he that is in you, than he that is in the world.

Romans 8;31 - What shall we then say to these things? If God be for us, who can be against us?

Jeremiah 30:17 - For I will restore health unto thee, and I will heal thee of thy wounds, saith the Lord; because they called thee an Outcast, saying, This is Zion, whom no man seeketh after.

Jeremiah 33:6 - Behold, I will bring it health and cure, and I will cure them, and will reveal unto them the abundance of peace and truth.

Psalm 41:3 - The Lord will strengthen him upon the bed of languishing: thou wilt make all his bed in his sickness.

In the NASB, this verse is translated to say that the Lord will sustain him upon his sickbed and restore him to health. What an awesome promise!

I Peter 2:24 - Who his own self bare our sins in his own body on the tree, that we, being dead to sins, should live unto righteousness: by whose stripes ye were healed.

Psalm 103:1-5 –

1 Bless the Lord, O my soul: and all that is within me, bless his holy name.

2 Bless the Lord, O my soul, and forget not all his benefits:

3 Who forgiveth all thine iniquities; who healeth all thy diseases;

4 Who redeemeth thy life from destruction; who crowneth thee with lovingkindness and tender mercies;

5 Who satisfieth thy mouth with good things; so that thy youth is renewed like the eagle's.

Psalm 107:20 - He sent his word, and healed them, and delivered them from their destructions.

Psalm 118:17 - I shall not die, but live, and declare the works of the Lord.

Psalm 30:2 - O Lord my God, I cried unto thee, and thou hast healed me.

Psalm 35:27 - Let them shout for joy, and be glad, that favour my righteous cause: yea, let them say continually, Let the Lord be magnified, which hath pleasure in the prosperity of his servant.

Psalm 119:50 - My soul breaketh for the longing that it hath unto thy judgments at all times.

3 John 1:2 - Beloved, I wish above all things that thou mayest prosper and be in health, even as thy soul prospereth.Jeremiah 17:14 - heal me o lord

II Corinthians 1:20 - For all the promises of God in him are yea, and in him Amen, unto the glory of God by us.

Exodus 23:25 - And ye shall serve the Lord your God, and he shall bless thy bread, and thy water; and I will take sickness away from the midst of thee.

Deuteronomy 30:19 - I call heaven and earth to record this day against you, that I have set before you life and death, blessing and cursing: therefore choose life, that both thou and thy seed may live:

Matthew 18:18 - Verily I say unto you, Whatsoever ye shall bind on earth shall be bound in heaven: and whatsoever ye shall loose on earth shall be loosed in heaven.

Mark 11:22-23 -

22 And Jesus answering saith unto them, Have faith in God.

23 For verily I say unto you, That whosoever shall say unto this mountain, Be thou removed, and be thou cast into the sea; and shall not doubt in his heart, but shall believe that those things which he saith shall come to pass; he shall have whatsoever he saith.

Hebrews 10:23 - Let us hold fast the profession of our faith without wavering; (for he is faithful that promised;)

2 Corinthians 12:9 - And he said unto me, My grace is sufficient for thee: for my strength is made perfect in weakness. Most gladly therefore will I rather glory in my infirmities, that the power of Christ may rest upon me.

Joel 3:10 - Beat your plowshares into swords and your pruninghooks into spears: let the weak say, I am strong.

Luke 12:32 - Fear not, little flock; for it is your Father's good pleasure to give you the kingdom.

Psalm 35:27 - Let them shout for joy, and be glad, that favour my righteous cause: yea, let them say continually, Let the Lord be magnified, which hath pleasure in the prosperity of his servant.

Nahum 1:9 - What do ye imagine against the LORD? he will make an utter end: affliction shall not rise up the second time.

Jeremiah 29:11 - For I know the thoughts that I think toward you, saith the Lord, thoughts of peace, and not of evil, to give you an expected end.

Proverbs 4:20-22 –

20 My son, attend to my words; incline thine ear unto my sayings.

21 Let them not depart from thine eyes; keep them in the midst of thine heart.

22 For they are life unto those that find them, and health to all their flesh.

Psalm 34:19 - Many are the afflictions of the righteous: but the Lord delivereth him out of them all.

Isaiah 41:10 - Fear thou not; for I am with thee: be not dismayed; for I am thy God: I will strengthen thee; yea, I will help thee; yea, I will uphold thee with the right hand of my righteousness.

Isaiah 54:17 - No weapon that is formed against thee shall prosper; and every tongue that shall rise against thee in judgment thou shalt condemn. This is the heritage of the servants of the Lord, and their righteousness is of me, saith the Lord.

Proverbs 12:6 - The words of the wicked are to lie in wait for blood: but the mouth of the upright shall deliver them.

Proverbs 12:18 - There is that speaketh like the piercings of a sword: but the tongue of the wise is health.

Proverbs 17:22 - A merry heart doeth good like a medicine: but a broken spirit drieth the bones.

Proverbs 18:7 - A fool's mouth is his destruction, and his lips are the snare of his soul.

1. **Get the Revelation.** The first step had been to get a revelation of the truth that God really did want me well. There's no point in starting your healing journey until you understand deep in your spirit that God really does desire for you to be healed, not sick, because if you do start it before that, the enemy will talk you into doubting, and you'll waver and receive nothing. Then the enemy will move in and attack you harder to try to discourage you from trying again.

2. **Know Your Right to Healing.** The second step had been to determine I was entitled to healing as part of the covenant, as an eternal promise of God. I knew for sure I had a legal right to healing, and that I wasn't going against God's will. I had a clear path to healing from there. Nothing was left but to understand how to reach out and take it.

3. **Declare the Symptoms are Lies.** The third step would be to declare the symptoms and sickness and disease a lie and cast down every imagination that came with them, while declaring the truth out loud, over and over, until it manifested itself in every part of my body, driving out the darkness of sickness and pain as it did so.

4. **Stand in Spite of Repeated Attacks.** The fourth step was standing in the face of repeated and increased attacks, knowing the victory had already been won, and refusing to back down.

5. **Attack the Symptoms – Hard.** I continued to attack every symptom and every pain with the power of the Word of God, and declaring the pain and anything else the enemy brought were not mine, and I wasn't keeping them, regardless of what the doctor declared about no cure, or this or that.

6. **Reprogram Your Mind Screen.** Our minds command our bodies. That means if I can't get the picture on my mind screen, I can't produce the command for my body to follow. I realized then that

there was no use in going any further until I could see myself healed in my mind.

The image in our mind is the "believe" part of Mark 11:23-24, tearing down the lies and unbelief sickness and pain had established!

Mark 11:23-24

For verily I say unto you, That whosoever shall say unto this mountain, Be thou removed, and be thou cast into the sea; and shall not doubt in his heart, but shall believe that those things which he saith shall come to pass; he shall have whatsoever he saith.

Therefore I say unto you, What things soever ye desire, when ye pray, believe that ye receive them, and ye shall have them.

Me – August 2014

EPILOGUE

My healing journey has lasted years and been very painful, but it is nothing compared to many of yours.

It is my hope that in reading this book and applying the principles contained herein that your journey will be much shorter, and much easier.

Walking my two dogs today, as I breathed in the fresh evening air, I really delighted in knowing that healing truly is mine now, and no devil in hell can take it from me. Sickness and pain – gone forever! It is truly a joyous thought, and I cannot stop praising God for it, and for making it so available to every single one of His children.

May you never be the same after reading *The Healing*

Companion, and may you walk in radiant and joyful health forevermore.

God bless you – now and always,

Glynda Lomax

Be still and know that I am God. ~ Ps 46:10

Glynda Lomax is a Christian author, Youtuber and podcaster. She is the host of Just Praise Him Radio on Podbean.com sharing prophetic messages, visions and the Word of God to inspire others to a closer walk with Christ. Glynda maintains a prophetic word blog at wingsofprophecy.blogspot.com that spiritually feeds tens of thousands of Christians around the world.

Glynda has committed her life to spreading the gospel of Jesus Christ. She currently resides in the Ozark Mountains of Northern Arkansas with her two very bossy dogs, where she is currently planning her next book.

Glynda is the author of a number of Christian books. All her print books and Kindle eBooks are available at www.amazon.com and at her website,www.justpraisehim.today. Many of her books are also available in audio book versions at Audible.com where new members can get one free audiobook when they join. (as of May 2019).

Wings of Prophecy – From the Beginning

What is God saying to His people, to the Church in America, and to this nation as a whole? How close are we to the end of this Age as we know it, and what events will tell us when we are in it? What special instructions and observations does God have for those who want to be included in the Bride of Jesus Christ? Where does the Rapture fit into all of this? These questions and many more will be addressed in Wings of Prophecy - From the Beginning

The Wilderness Companion – Glynda's Signature Message

Every Christian must pass through the desert on the way to their Promised Land. Wilderness experiences are often times of great uncertainty and change. Our time in the desert seasons of our lives is lengthened or shortened depending on our response to each circumstance. Our faith in Christ is refined in the intense heat of the desert experience as our intimacy with Him increases. Find out how to go from surviving to thriving by partnering with God as He leads you in the path that will strengthen your faith and prepare you to step into your destiny. The Wilderness Companion will help you.

Loosed from Chains of Darkness – Destroying Curses through the Power of the Cross

Are there areas of your life you just can't seem to overcome in, no matter what you try? Are you plagued by depression, poverty, anger, lust, or failure? Do you recognize your predisposition to commit the same sins committed by your forefathers? Do you want a better life?

Many people live their whole lives under generational and other types of curses without understanding they can be free. Learn what the scriptures say about curses and why they are still relevant today. Learn how to defeat every one through the power of the Cross of Jesus Christ.

Hosea 4:6 My people are destroyed for lack of knowledge: because thou hast rejected knowledge, I will also reject thee, that thou shalt be no priest to me: seeing thou hast forgotten the law of thy God, I will also forget thy children.

If you have the knowledge, you can break the curses off your life and start experiencing breakthroughs like never before.

In this book, you will learn the basics of four different types of curses, plus how to break these specific curses: • Abuse – a curse that causes people to abuse you or you to abuse others • Anger – a curse that causes angry outbursts and constant anger • Barrenness – a curse that causes miscarriages and prevents pregnancies • Captivity – a curse that causes addictions, incarcerations, traps • Depression – a curse that brings a plague of depression • Divorce and Division – a curse that causes severed relationships • Failure – causes you to fail over and over in your endeavors • Fear – a curse that brings a plague of fears and anxieties • Freemasonry – a myriad of curses caused by involvement in Freemasonry • Illegitimacy – a curse that causes lust, rebellion and sexual dysfunction • Infirmity – a curse that causes moral weaknesses and sickness after sickness • Innocent Blood – a curse that causes the death of innocent people in your line • Lust – a plague of lust • Perversion – causes ongoing problems with perverse thoughts and actions • Poverty – a curse that prevents prosperity, no matter how hard you work • PTSD – a curse that plagues you with nightmares and flashbacks • Vagabond – a curse that causes wandering, aimlessness and lawlessness.

You can contact Glynda at:

wingsofprophecy@gmail.com

or write to her by mail at:

Glynda Lomax
P.O. Box 60
Glencoe, AR 72539-0060

My Healing Scriptures:

NOTES:

Made in United States
North Haven, CT
10 June 2024

53437051R00104